D1162971

THE
ARTIFICIAL
HEART

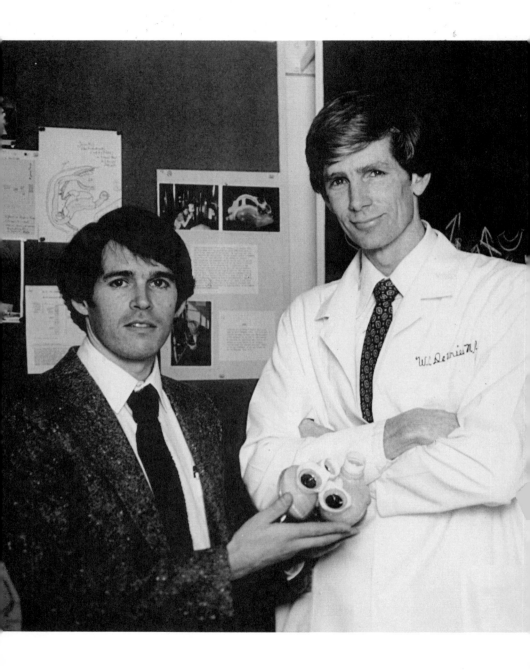

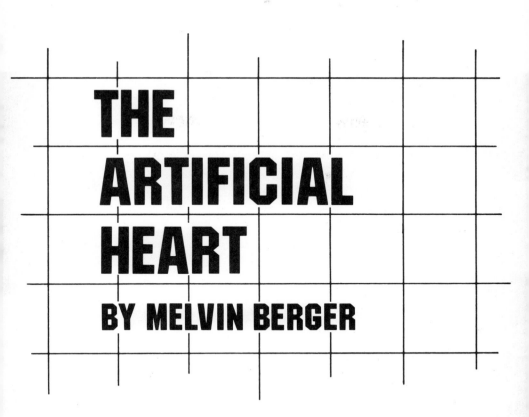

THE ARTIFICIAL HEART

BY MELVIN BERGER

ILLUSTRATIONS BY ANNE CANEVARI GREEN

A GROLIER COMPANY

FRANKLIN WATTS
NEW YORK LONDON TORONTO SYDNEY 1987
AN IMPACT BOOK

FRONTIS: DRS. JARVIK (LEFT) AND DEVRIES,
WITH THE JARVIK-7 ARTIFICIAL HEART

Photographs courtesy of Photo Researchers, Inc.: pp. 2 & 51 (Hank Morgan),
15 (Morris Huberland), 19 (George Whiteley), 25 (Dr. Tony Brain/ Science
Photo Library), 41 (Bruce Roberts); University of Utah Medical Center,
photos by Brad Nelson: 8, 53, 61, 63, 65; UPI/Bettmann Newsphotos: pp. 12
(top), 30, 48, 96; Cardiovascular Associates, Texas Heart Institute, Houston.
Courtesy Denton A. Cooley, M.D.: pp. 12 (bottom), 73; American Heart
Association: p. 22; AP/Wide World Photos: pp. 35, 54, 76, 109; News Office,
Massachusetts General Hospital, Boston: p. 40; University of Utah: p. 45;
Rothco: pp. 56 (Mike Luckovich, The Greenville News), 80 (Linda Boileau,
Frankfort State Journal, Kentucky), 113 (Dennis Renault, Sacramento Bee,
California); Black Star, photos by William Strode: pp. 69, 88, 105.

Library of Congress Cataloging-in-Publication Data

Berger, Melvin.
The artificial heart.

(An Impact book)
Bibliography: p.
Includes index.
Summary: Traces the history of the development of the
artificial heart, including experimentation with animal
and human heart transplants, and discusses the psychological and ethical issues surrounding their use.
1. Heart, Artificial—History—Juvenile literature
2. Heart, Artificial—Moral and ethical aspects—Juvenile
literature.   3. Heart, Artificial—Psychological aspects—
Juvenile literature. [1. Heart, Artificial]   I. Title.
RD598.35.A78B47   1987   617'.412059   87-6241
ISBN 0-531-10409-5

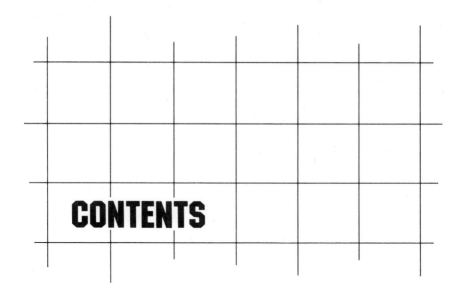

CONTENTS

THE
ARTIFICIAL
HEART

*The operating room at the University of
Utah Medical Center, during the implantof
an artificial heart in recipient Barney Clark*

1

INTRODUCTION

It was shortly after midnight on the cold, snowy morning of December 2, 1982. The place was Operating Room 4 of the University of Utah Medical Center in Salt Lake City, Utah. The patient was a sixty-one-year-old retired dentist, Barney Clark. The chief surgeon was Dr. William C. DeVries, thirty-eight years old. The event was one of the most dramatic moments in the entire history of medicine. For the first time ever, a surgeon was removing the diseased heart of a living person and replacing it with a permanent, mechanical, artificial heart.

When Barney Clark was wheeled into the operating room he was suffering from a fatal heart disease and was near death. For seven-and-a-half hours, Dr. DeVries and the surgical team labored to implant the first artificial heart in Clark's chest. The device was designed to take the place of his heart and to last forever.

Barney Clark lived for nearly four months on his artificial heart. During that time he remained attached by long tubes to the heart driver, a unit the size of a washing machine, which supplied the compressed air to power his artificial heart. He was never able to leave the hospital.

And he was troubled by medical complications ranging from strokes to severe nosebleeds that could not be stopped. There were times Clark said he wanted to die. But more often he insisted that he had made the right choice and that his ordeal was worth it.

Some compare Barney Clark and Dr. DeVries to Christopher Columbus making a voyage of discovery through uncharted waters. Surely their journey was just as difficult and their goal no less remarkable. By implanting a permanent, total artificial heart into a human being, Dr. DeVries opened a whole new frontier in medicine.

Others, however, point out that the implantation of the artificial heart in Barney Clark's chest came at the end of many years of research and experimentation by scores of scientists at medical centers all around the country. And they question the success of an operation that sustained the patient for only four months.

ANCIENT TIMES

The idea of replacing a diseased or damaged human body part goes back nearly four thousand years. In the early efforts tissue from one's own body or that from another person was used. Writings from ancient Egypt tell about warriors whose faces were disfigured in battle. These injured soldiers had skin grafted from other parts of their bodies to their faces to improve their appearance.

The primitive physicians who did these skin grafts were merely following an even older agricultural practice. Farmers long knew that you could dig up a living plant, move it to another location, place it in the earth—and the plant would grow in the new spot.

The name for this procedure—transplant—came to be applied to the replacement of human body parts. The source could be the individual's own body, as with the skin graft. Or it could be the body of someone who just died or a donor who gave up a body part, such as a second kidney.

HEART REPLACEMENTS

The modern idea of replacing the human heart can be traced back to 1812. In that year a French scientist, Julian Jean César La Gallois, first suggested that a continuing injection of blood could maintain life for someone whose heart had failed.

Since then, many doctors and scientists have worked to create a mechanical device to take the place of the heart for pumping blood. In 1880 Henry Martin built his "heart-lung preparation," a machine to pump blood through those organs. In 1928 H. H. Dale and E. H. J. Schuster announced that they had built a pump that could circulate the blood of a "heartless animal." The most famous early heart machine was the so-called Lindbergh pump of the 1930s, designed by Charles Lindbergh, the well-known aviation pioneer, and Alexis Carrel, a prominent surgeon and researcher. An experimental mechanical heart built by F. D. Dodrill of the Research Division of General Motors in 1952 was used to keep a patient alive for nearly an hour during surgery on his heart. Since 1953 heart-lung machines have become necessary pieces of equipment in operating rooms where open-heart surgery is performed.

While some researchers were developing the hardware of an artificial heart, others were at work at improving the medical and surgical skills necessary to replace a human heart. Alexis Carrel made major contributions in both areas. In 1905, working with Dr. Charles Guthries, he was studying ways to suture, or stitch, blood vessels together. They developed a new technique to connect blood vessels and eliminate bleeding.

With their new method, Carrel and Guthrie performed the very first heart transplant. They removed a heart from one dog and transplanted it into another. But they did not remove the second dog's heart. They left it in place and attached the transplanted heart to blood vessels in its neck.

The transplanted heart functioned well for about two hours. Then a blood clot formed and the dog died.

[11]

Right: Dr. Christiaan Barnard, South African heart transplant specialist who performed the world's first heart transplant

Below: This is a model of the first artificial heart implanted in a human, on April 4, 1969, at the Texas Heart Institute.

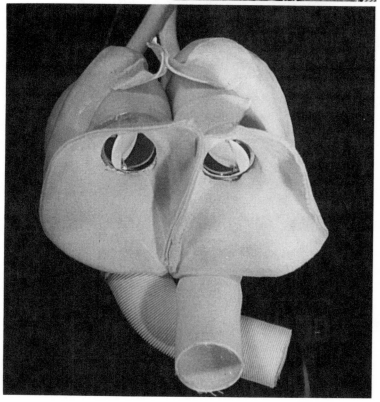

Many advances in the understanding and techniques of heart transplantation occurred over the following decades. But surely none was greater than the breakthrough that came in 1967. That year Dr. Christiaan Barnard did the first transplantation of a human heart. Thousands of human heart transplants have followed Dr. Barnard's historic achievement.

Still, scientists searched for an artificial heart that could take the place of the diseased heart within the patient's body. After many years of animal experimentation, Dr. Denton A. Cooley made the first implant of an artificial heart into a human patient in 1969. The device was a temporary, emergency unit, meant only to keep the patient alive until a human heart donor could be found. It worked perfectly for sixty-four hours, at which time a donor heart was located. Although many felt the heart was not yet ready for human use, this first implantation showed that artificial hearts could indeed work.

Since 1982, when Barney Clark received the first permanent artificial heart, much has been learned. The first few artificial hearts were used as permanent replacements for diseased hearts. More recently, though, the artificial hearts are being used to keep seriously ill patients alive until they can get human heart transplants.

The struggle to perfect the artificial heart and the technique of implantation has been accompanied by a search for answers to a host of ethical and moral questions. The problems range all the way from who should decide who gets the transplants and implants (since there are not nearly enough to go around), to who should pay for these extremely expensive forms of treatment.

In the following chapters we'll explore the entire subject of the heart and modern medicine, starting with a look at the healthy human heart and heart transplants. Then we will survey the development of the artificial heart, including the procedures used to implant the device, early patients, main uses of the device, and the many perplexing issues raised by the modern-day artificial heart.

[13]

2

THE HUMAN

HEART

People think of the heart as the core of their being—the source of their feelings and emotions. Affection is a "warm heart" and disappointment in love is a "broken heart." Sadness is a "heavy heart" or being "sick at heart." Fear is a "faint heart" or having your "heart in your mouth." An intimate conversation is "heart to heart." "Cross my heart" is a solemn oath. "Heart of iron" means brave and courageous; "heart of stone" means cruel and mean. And to wear one's "heart on one's sleeve" is to have no secrets.

But to doctors and scientists the heart is much more. The heart is also an extraordinary muscle that works as a pump. The heart itself is hollow. But the heart muscles beat, or contract, about 40 million times a year. They pump more than 5 quarts (4.5 l) of blood per minute through some 100,000 miles (160,000 km) of blood vessels in every part of the body.

On the journey from the heart to the rest of the body, the blood carries oxygen to the body's cells. This oxygen gives the cells the ability to grow and function. On the way back to the heart, the blood takes away the cell's wastes, such as carbon dioxide. After passing through the heart, the blood goes to the lungs. Here it gets rid of the carbon dioxide and picks up a fresh supply of oxygen. Then it returns to the heart, ready to be pumped out for a trip around the body once again.

HOW IT WORKS

The heart is a hard-working organ. Day and night, weekday or weekend, it beats sixty to eighty times a minute. If it stops for just a few seconds the person becomes unconscious. If it stops for five minutes the person is "brain dead."

Despite its heavy load, the heart is quite small. Each person's heart is a little bigger than his or her fist. Children have small hearts that become larger as they get older. A full-grown heart weighs about 10 ounces (280 g).

Most people think that the heart is on the left side of the chest. Actually, it is located near the center of the chest, right between the lungs. The lower part, though, points

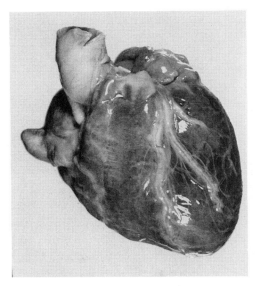

A normal, healthy human heart

THE HEART
Front view

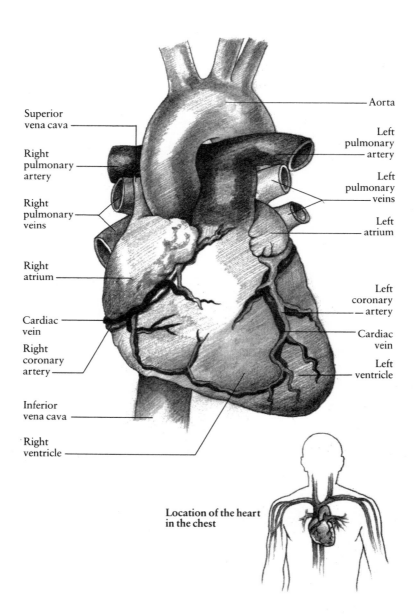

Aorta

Superior vena cava

Right pulmonary artery

Right pulmonary veins

Right atrium

Cardiac vein

Right coronary artery

Inferior vena cava

Right ventricle

Left pulmonary artery

Left pulmonary veins

Left atrium

Left coronary artery

Cardiac vein

Left ventricle

Location of the heart in the chest

THE HEART
Rear view

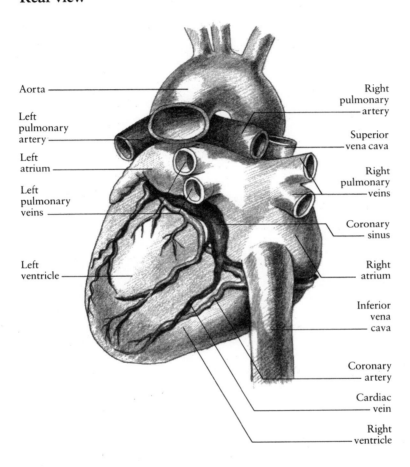

Aorta

Left pulmonary artery

Left atrium

Left pulmonary veins

Left ventricle

Right pulmonary artery

Superior vena cava

Right pulmonary veins

Coronary sinus

Right atrium

Inferior vena cava

Coronary artery

Cardiac vein

Right ventricle

The blood vessels

Artery   Vein   Capillary

THE HEART
Cross section

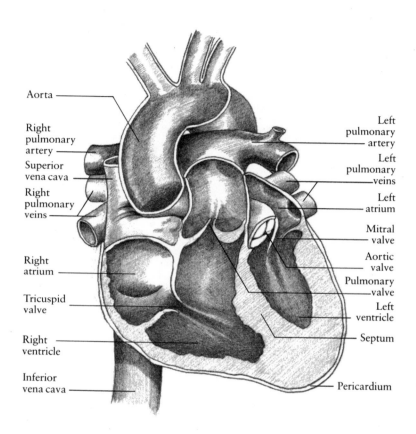

Aorta

Right pulmonary artery

Superior vena cava

Right pulmonary veins

Right atrium

Tricuspid valve

Right ventricle

Inferior vena cava

Left pulmonary artery

Left pulmonary veins

Left atrium

Mitral valve

Aortic valve

Pulmonary valve

Left ventricle

Septum

Pericardium

A heart beat

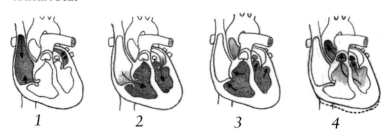

1   2   3   4

*Cardiac muscle in the left
ventricle area of the heart*

off to the left. Because it is the lower portion of the heart
that you can feel beating, the entire heart is mistakenly
believed to be located there.

The heart is enclosed in a thin covering called the pericardium. The pericardium is a tough lining that protects
the heart from rubbing against the lungs and chest wall.

An up-and-down wall of muscle, the septum, divides
the heart in half. There are two chambers, one above the
other, on each side of the heart. The upper chamber on
each side is called the atrium (plural, *atria*). The atria receive the blood flowing back to the heart. The lower chambers are the ventricles. They pump the blood out from the
heart.

[19]

The walls of the atria are thin compared to those of the ventricles. The right ventricle wall is rather thick. It must be able to contract and force the blood up to the lungs. But the wall of the left ventricle is even thicker—about three times the thickness of the right ventricle. The left ventricle pumps the blood throughout the entire body.

The vessels that carry blood away from the heart are the arteries. The vessels through which the blood flows back to the heart are the veins.

In general, the right atrium and ventricle get the blood from the veins and pump it to the lungs to pick up oxygen. The left atrium and ventricle get the blood from the lungs and pump it to the body. The arteries usually carry oxygen-rich blood to the cells and the veins usually carry oxygen-poor blood back to the heart. The exceptions are the arteries from the heart to the lungs, which carry blood containing carbon dioxide, and the veins from the lungs to the heart, which have just picked up oxygen in the lungs.

CIRCULATION

Let's trace some blood as it moves through the body. We start where the blood flows through a vein and into the heart. The blood enters the right atrium through two veins called the vena cava. The superior vena cava brings blood from the upper body—the head and arms. The inferior vena cava's blood comes from the lower body—the trunk and legs.

The right atrium fills with blood. The muscles that make up its walls contract. This forces the blood out through the tricuspid valve down into the right ventricle. The tricuspid and other valves control the flow of the blood. They allow it to move in only one direction and prevent it from backing up.

The right ventricle then fills with blood. Its muscles contract. The tightening of the muscles squeezes the blood through another valve, the pulmonary valve, into the pul-

THE CIRCULATORY SYSTEM

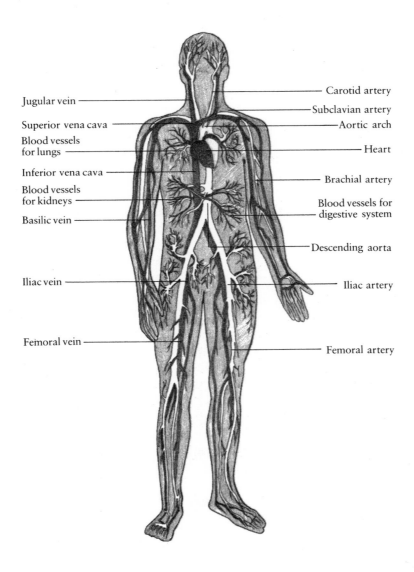

Jugular vein

Superior vena cava

Blood vessels
for lungs

Inferior vena cava

Blood vessels
for kidneys

Basilic vein

Iliac vein

Femoral vein

Carotid artery

Subclavian artery

Aortic arch

Heart

Brachial artery

Blood vessels for
digestive system

Descending aorta

Iliac artery

Femoral artery

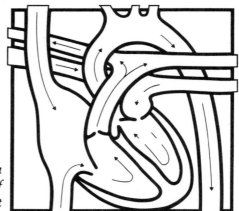

A schematic diagram
showing the flow of
blood through the heart

monary artery. The blood is pushed by the heart through the pulmonary artery to the lungs. As the blood passes through the blood vessels in the lungs, the carbon dioxide passes out through the thin walls of the blood vessels. The person breathes out, or exhales, the carbon dioxide. Then, when he or she breathes in, or inhales, the blood picks up a fresh supply of oxygen through the blood vessel walls.

The oxygen-rich blood flows back to the heart. It enters the left atrium through the four pulmonary veins. The walls of the left atrium contract, sending the blood through the mitral valve down into the left ventricle. The left ventricle is the primary pumping station of the heart. It has the heaviest, strongest muscle walls. Each time the left ventricle contracts, the person feels it as a heartbeat. The powerful pumping action of the left ventricle sends the blood pulsing out through the aortic valve into the aorta.

The aorta is the main artery of the body. It runs in an up-and-down direction. Smaller arteries branch off from the aorta to different parts of the body. Coming out of these smaller arteries are still smaller blood vessels, called arterioles. Finally, hair-thin capillaries bring the blood to

RESPIRATION

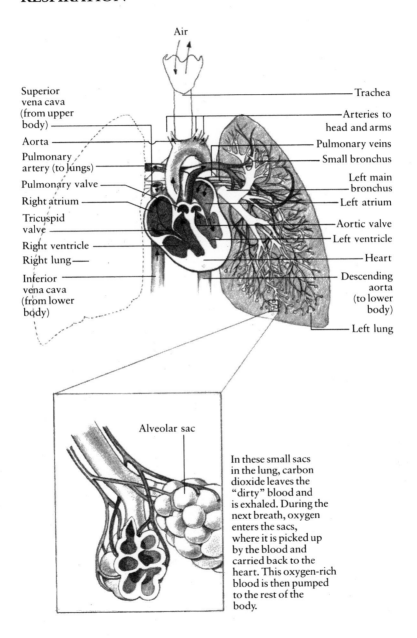

Air

Superior vena cava (from upper body)

Aorta

Pulmonary artery (to lungs)

Pulmonary valve

Right atrium

Tricuspid valve

Right ventricle

Right lung

Inferior vena cava (from lower body)

Trachea

Arteries to head and arms

Pulmonary veins

Small bronchus

Left main bronchus

Left atrium

Aortic valve

Left ventricle

Heart

Descending aorta (to lower body)

Left lung

Alveolar sac

In these small sacs in the lung, carbon dioxide leaves the "dirty" blood and is exhaled. During the next breath, oxygen enters the sacs, where it is picked up by the blood and carried back to the heart. This oxygen-rich blood is then pumped to the rest of the body.

every corner of the body, from the tips of the toes to the top of the head.

On the blood's journey, the red blood cells bring oxygen to the body cells. At the same time they pick up the carbon dioxide that the body cells produce. The blood then proceeds back to the heart through the capillaries, venules (small veins), and veins. It enters the right atrium through the superior vena cava and inferior vena cava. And the process starts all over again—as it does from the moment of birth to the instant of death.

The circulating blood, though, does more than just carry oxygen to the body cells and carbon dioxide to the lungs. The blood also brings the cells the nutrients, such as fats, sugars, and other energy sources, which they need. And it removes the waste products that the cells produce.

WHEN SOMETHING GOES WRONG

Sometimes one step of this complicated sequence of events does not take place as it should. One million deaths—half of all those in the United States every year—are caused by something going wrong with the functioning of the heart or circulation system. In addition, the American Heart Association estimates that approximately 63 million Americans, about one out of every four, suffer from some defect, disease, or damage to the heart.

The blockage of a blood vessel is an extremely common problem. Two main causes are a buildup of fatty deposits (called atherosclerosis) or a blood clot (thrombosis). When this happens in a coronary artery—an artery that supplies blood to the heart itself—the result can be angina pectoris, a sharp pain in the chest. When the blockage is more serious the person suffers a heart attack, with intense, crushing pain, nausea, and difficulty in breathing. Doctors call this a myocardial infarction. The term refers to the fact that the heart muscle is suffering from a lack of oxygen.

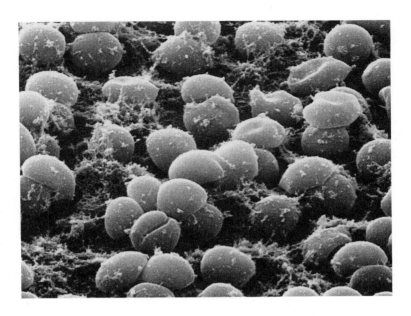

*This scanning electron micrograph shows
red blood cells trapped in a blood clot.*

Some infants are born with a heart that is not correctly
formed. In many of these so-called blue babies, the blood
passes directly from the right to the left side of the heart
without going through the lungs. The lack of oxygen from
the lungs gives the baby's skin a bluish tinge. If uncorrected,
this condition leads to death.

Rheumatic fever is a childhood disease that can damage
the heart valves so that they do not work properly. There
are many other diseases and infections as well that attack
the heart muscles or valves. In most of these conditions
the person becomes very weak or suffers a good deal of
pain and discomfort.

Some heart deficiencies can be treated with drugs. Other
conditions can be corrected or improved by surgery. De-
fective valves can be repaired or replaced. Blocked coro-

nary arteries can be treated by bypass surgery. In this procedure, the clogged artery is bypassed by a vein the surgeon has removed from the patient's leg or by an artery from the chest wall.

But what happens when the doctors have no medical or surgical way to improve a heart patient's condition? That is when they may turn to the most extreme treatment—either a human heart transplant or an artificial heart implant.

3

HUMAN HEART TRANSPLANTS

The patient has terminal heart disease and is rapidly approaching death. Doctors have used many different drugs and various types of equipment to try to save his failing heart. Nothing has helped. Day by day the patient grows weaker. The doctors have only one hope of saving him. They will perform a heart transplant. They will replace his damaged heart with a healthy heart from someone who has just died.

A young man is brought into the emergency room of the same hospital. Twenty-two-years-old and in excellent health, he had been riding his motorcycle without a helmet. A skid sent him headlong into the side of a building. All activity in his brain has stopped. He is legally dead. His heart continues to beat only because he is hooked up to a respirator, which breathes for him.

The doctors speak with the young man's relatives. They ask for permission to transplant the dead man's heart into the body of the very sick patient. Immediately after the family grants the request, the doctors perform the operation. They attach the heart from the dead man, the donor

*heart, in the body of the patient, the recipient. Within
moments the heart in the recipient's chest is beating and
pumping blood. His life is saved.*

Although this isn't an actual story, it is typical of the more
than nine hundred heart transplants that will be done this
year. Almost all will be successful. They will add years of
life to patients who would otherwise have died in days or
weeks.

THE OPERATION

The transplantation of a human heart may sound like the
most difficult and demanding of all kinds of surgery. Yet
doctors say a heart transplant is simpler than many other
surgical procedures. Some consider it easier than a liver
transplant, since fewer blood vessel connections have to
be made. To Dr. Norman Shumway, a leading heart surgeon, a heart transplant is "sort of like sewing up a hole
in a pair of socks."

Simply described, doctors first cut through the skin,
bone, and other tissue to expose the heart. Next they hook
the patient up to a heart-lung machine. All of the work of
the patient's heart during surgery will be taken over by this
device.

The surgeons next remove most of the disabled heart.
Usually they leave in place the atria and the veins leading
to the atria. But they cut away the two ventricles, which
are the main pumping chambers of the heart.

While this operation is going on, or shortly before, the
heart to be transplanted is prepared. The donor heart usually comes from an otherwise healthy person who is killed
in a serious accident. Or it comes from someone who died
of a fatal disease that did not affect the heart. Since the
heart cannot exist outside a living body for more than
about four hours, the doctors must work fast to transplant
the donor heart as quickly as possible.

[28]

In the past, it was easy to know when someone died. This was the moment when the person stopped breathing. Now it is more difficult. With respirators that actually breathe for the person, the distinction between life and death is not so clear. For that reason, doctors and government authorities use a new legal definition of death to guide their actions.

The definition states that a person is dead when he or she is in a coma and cannot be roused, does not respond to any form of stimulation, cannot breathe without a respirator, has no reflexes, and shows no sign of electrical activity in the brain.

The donor heart must be similar to the recipient's heart if a transplant is to be successful. The first consideration is size. Is the heart the right dimension for the recipient? An adult man's heart will not fit into the chest of an infant. And a child's heart cannot pump enough blood to meet the needs of a grown-up.

Then, blood type must be considered. Do donor and recipient match in this respect? One of the big dangers of transplantation is the rejection reaction. That is, the recipient's body responds to the transplanted organ as an invader and attacks the heart in an effort to protect itself. Rejection proved to be the major problem in the early transplants. But now doctors know that rejection is less likely to occur if the donor's blood closely matches that of the recipient.

With a well-matched donor heart at hand, the surgeons can go ahead with the transplant. They carefully place the new heart in the recipient's chest and suture it to the remaining walls of the atria and to the aorta and pulmonary artery. Then there is that magical moment when the new heart starts to beat on its own. Finally, the patient is removed from the heart-lung machine.

From this point on, the transplanted heart works like a healthy heart. The chest cavity is closed and recovery begins.

Jim Hayes (right) pedals into Stanford Medical Center for a checkup on the transplanted heart he received five years earlier. It was the end of a 2,800-mile (4,480-km) trek across the country by bicycle. His brother, Dewayne, is the other cyclist.

When fully healed, the person can resume activity and lead almost a normal life. In a remarkable example of heart transplant achievement, Jim Hayes, age thirty-three, rode his bicycle 2,800 miles (4,480 km) from his home in Tennessee to the Stanford University Medical Center in California for his fifth annual posttransplant checkup!

THE FOLLOW-UP

The job of fighting off the body's rejection of the new heart never ends. It goes on as long as the recipient lives.

Doctors used to prescribe a variety of drugs to stop the rejection reaction. These drugs suppressed, or checked, the body's immune system, which sends out cells to attack invaders, such as disease-causing bacteria and viruses. Unfortunately, the drugs not only suppressed the immune system, they also robbed the body of its ability to fight off infection. As a result, although the transplanted heart was not rejected, the patients fell victim to all sorts of sicknesses.

Today, doctors have a new drug, cyclosporine, which works to suppress the immune system but without destroying the body's ability to fight infection. Since a rejection reaction is always possible, patients must take the drug every day for life. Transplant surgeon Dr. Thomas Starzl of the University of Colorado Medical Center calls cyclosporine "the key that unlocks the door to transplants."

From the time cyclosporine began to be used, in 1980, it has made possible an increasing number of transplantations. In that year, only 36 transplants were done in the United States. With cyclosporine the numbers began moving up. In 1981 there were 62; in 1982 there were 103; in 1983 there were 172; in 1984 there were 350; in 1985 there were 730; in 1986 there were nearly 1,000—and the figures are still rising.

The results have also been getting better and better. Around 80 percent of all heart transplant recipients have survived at least one year, 60 percent have survived for three years, and 40 percent have survived for five years. The success rate far surpasses any other method of treatment for end-stage heart disease. Over 95 percent of the recipients have achieved "Class I" status. This is a measurement that cardiologists use. It means that the person has no physical limitations. More than 80 percent have returned to work and are leading normal lives.

In the United States the longest survival on record is Willem Van Buuren of San Rafael, California. Van Buuren received his new—but used—heart in 1970 and is still thriving. The world record, though, belongs to Emmanuel Vitra of Marseilles, France, who lives with a transplanted heart that he received in 1968.

SOME BACKGROUND

Heart transplantation became a reality for the first time in 1905 with the historic dog heart transplant of Carrel and Guthrie. Over the following years a number of animal heart transplants were done. The donor hearts were placed in the neck, the abdomen, and the chest cavity of the recipient dogs. But no one dared to put them in the heart's normal place. The results were not too promising.

In 1959, however, Drs. Norman Shumway and Richard Lower of the Stanford Medical Center in Palo Alto, California, began experimenting with heart transplants. In the early 1960s the two doctors did a series of eight transplants on dogs, replacing the recipient's heart with a donor heart. Three were failures. But five of the dogs lived from six to twenty-one days with their new hearts.

A major advance in heart transplant came in January 1964. Dr. James Hardy of the University of Mississippi Medical Center transplanted a chimpanzee heart into the chest of a sixty-eight-year-old man whose heart was failing. At first the heart seemed to be functioning well. But trouble soon developed and the patient died two hours after surgery. The heart seemed too small and too weak to provide the blood circulation of an adult man.

By 1967, based on his successful animal transplants, Dr. Shumway felt ready to try the first human transplant. He wrote in the November 1967 *Journal of the American Medical Association* that his team was "on the threshold of clinical application."

But Shumway was outdone. On December 3, 1967, Dr. Christiaan Barnard performed the very first human heart transplant at the Groote Schuur Hospital in Cape Town, South Africa. A year earlier, Dr. Barnard had watched Dr. Lower perform dog heart transplants at the Medical College of Virginia and had done some of his own. Thus prepared, Dr. Barnard returned to South Africa to await a suitable opportunity to do a human heart transplant.

The chance Barnard was waiting for came when fifty-four-year-old Louis Washkansky was admitted to the hospital with end-stage heart disease. The patient was no longer able to stand without help; he could not even breathe easily while lying on his back. Dr. Barnard considered him a good candidate for a transplant. But the surgeon could do nothing until he had a donor heart.

After several days of waiting for an accident victim, Denise Darvall, age twenty-five, was brought to Groote Schuur Hospital. She had been struck by a speeding car that smashed her skull. Brain dead, but with a heart that was still beating, Darvall became the perfect donor for Washkansky.

With all the elements in place, Dr. Barnard proceeded with the operation. It went well. For two weeks Washkansky continued to make a fine recovery. Then complications set in. He died on the eighteenth day, not of heart failure but of pneumonia.

Even though Washkansky lived for only a short while after the transplantation, Dr. Barnard felt good about his decision to go ahead with the surgery. "I wouldn't like to call this operation an experiment," he later said. "It was treatment of a sick patient."

Dr. Barnard did his second heart transplant exactly one month later, on January 3, 1968. The patient was Philip

Blaiberg. Blaiberg lived for 593 days, over a year and a half, with his transplanted heart. His life was extended far beyond the time he would have lived with his badly diseased heart. The cause of death was probably the rejection of the heart by his body.

Philip Blaiberg's success increased interest in heart transplants. During 1968 there were 105 heart transplants worldwide. Sad to say, most of the patients died within days or months. Only forty-three were alive at the end of the year. The longest survival record was still held by Philip Blaiberg.

The medical profession, as well as the public at large, began to feel that transplantation was not reliable enough to be used as a treatment of choice. After reaching a peak of twenty-six transplantations worldwide in the month of November 1968, transplantation surgery just about came to a halt. For the following twelve years, the rate of transplants remained at a trickle.

Most heart transplant failures were caused by the rejection of the heart by the body. But in 1980, with the introduction of cyclosporine and the new techniques developed by Dr. Shumway and his co-workers, doctors began to consider transplantation again. They did thirty-six transplants that year, and the results were encouraging. Since then, the numbers have shot upward.

THE FUTURE

Doctors are constantly exploring new methods of transplantation. A particularly interesting approach was used by Dr. Leonard L. Bailey of the Loma Linda Medical Center in California on October 26, 1984. Fifteen days earlier an infant girl, known only as Baby Fae, had been born with a badly deformed heart. Despite the center's very best efforts, Baby Fae was sinking fast.

The doctors were desperate. No donor heart was available. In a final attempt to save the infant's life, the surgeons

[34]

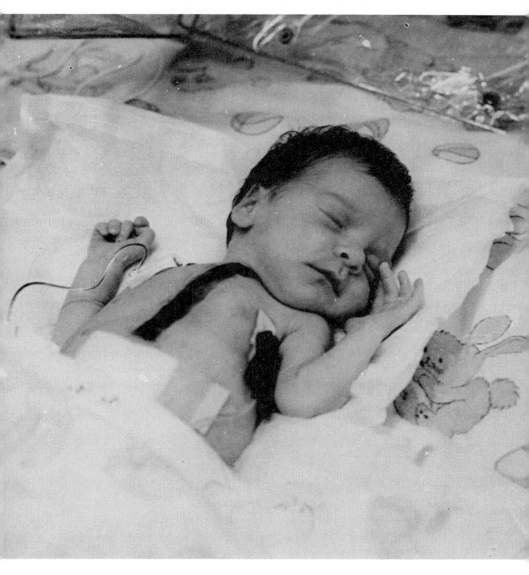

"Baby Fae," the infant recipient of a transplanted baboon's heart. Baby Fae lived for only a short while after the operation.

recalled the earlier experiments in which an animal heart was transplanted into a human. They decided to replace her bad heart with one from an animal. They transplanted a baboon's heart into her tiny chest. Unfortunately she did not survive for very long. But the experience showed that animal-to-human transplants were perhaps possible.

In another dramatic new development, researchers at the University of Pennsylvania in late 1986 fashioned a heart pump out of a dog's own back muscle and successfully implanted it in the dog. This procedure has many advantages over traditional implant and transplant procedures, including avoiding totally the risk of rejection and the need for a donor. Nor would the patient need to be tethered to outside power sources. It will undoubtedly be some time before doctors will be ready to try this procedure in a human.

The ever-improving success rate of human heart transplants is due mostly to gains in medical knowledge. Better matching of donor and recipient, as well as advanced surgical techniques, have boosted the survival rate. Giant strides have also been made in controlling rejection and the other complications that may arise after surgery. Perhaps most important now is the development of guidelines to determine who will be able to gain the most from a heart transplant.

These guidelines vary from hospital to hospital. But a good candidate for transplant is, in general, someone who

- has heart disease that offers the patient little hope of surviving beyond six months.
- is between thirteen and fifty years old.
- is relatively healthy, except for the heart disease.
- is able to cooperate with the doctors and is willing to follow a strict medical routine for the rest of his or her life.
- is psychologically stable.

A poor risk for transplantation is someone who

- has a serious disease or infection.
- is considerably overweight.
- has a history of mental illness.
- has a history of alcohol or drug abuse.

Despite the many successes, important questions remain. For example, what happens to good candidates for heart transplants for whom there are no donor hearts? Estimates of the number of people needing replacement hearts vary. According to Roger Evans of the Battelle Human Affairs Research Centers of Seattle, Washington, 15,000 to 50,000 patients every year could benefit from heart transplants. Dr. Willem Kolff of the University of Utah has given a higher estimate of between 60,000 and 100,000.

But everyone is in agreement on one point. The supply is much smaller than the demand. Dr. Norman Shumway offers his estimate of available donors with a quip: "There are more than 22,000 brain-dead people in the U.S. every year—not counting the legislators, of course." But Dwight Davis of the Milton S. Hershey Center in Hershey, Pennsylvania, believes that the total of available donor hearts is closer to about 3,000.

The many people in need of transplants, the scarcity of donor hearts, the staggering cost of each transplant, and the problem of having the patient, matching donor, and doctor together in the right place at the right time continue to hold back the program. About one-third of all transplant candidates die while waiting for a new heart.

For this reason, scientists have been trying to learn how to preserve hearts for periods of more than four hours. And in another avenue of research they are attempting to save the lives of patients with serious heart disease through the use of the artificial heart.

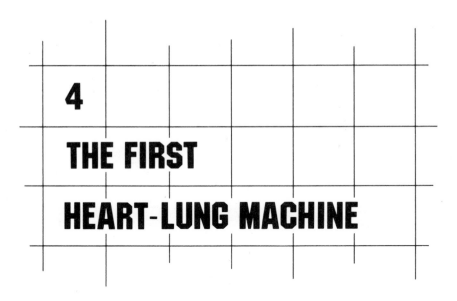

4

THE FIRST

HEART-LUNG MACHINE

The date: October 3, 1930.
The place: Massachusetts General Hospital, Boston.
The patient: Identified only as Edith S.

Edith S. had just had a routine gallbladder operation. She was recovering nicely when suddenly she felt a sharp pain in her chest. Her pulse became weak and rapid. Her blood pressure dropped way down. She could hardly breathe.

The doctors who rushed to her side came up with this diagnosis: A blood clot had formed during or after the operation. It was now blocking the pulmonary artery, the one that carries blood from the heart to the lungs. So far, some blood was able to squeeze past the clot. But if the blockage became complete she would die.

The doctors needed to operate on her heart and remove the clot. But to do so was extremely dangerous. Between the years 1912 and 1930, operations to remove blood clots from the heart had been tried 141 times. Only eight patients had survived. Surgery on the heart was an extremely risky business.

With that dismal history in mind, Edith's surgeon decided to wait. With luck the clot might break up by itself. Then the small clumps of blood cells would be washed away by the blood flow and clear the artery. But if the clot completely blocked the artery—for even a few minutes— the result would be permanent brain damage or death.

The surgeon moved Edith to an operating room. If her condition worsened, surgery could begin in seconds. From the instant her circulation was cut off, he would have six minutes to operate and remove the clot. The surgeon assigned young Dr. John Gibbon to watch over the patient. Dr. Gibbon was to sound the alarm as soon as he noticed any change in her status.

AN IDEA IS BORN

For seventeen hours Dr. Gibbon kept his eyes on the monitors tracking Edith's vital signs. As the time passed he found himself thinking that her life depended on an operation that had almost no chance of success. Was there any way to give her, and those with similar problems, better odds to live?

Dr. Gibbon understood the problem. Whenever doctors needed to operate on the heart, they had to do so without interfering with its work. This prevented them from doing all but the simplest of procedures. And they always had to move at top speed to avoid stopping the heartbeat for more than a few minutes.

So Dr. Gibbon began to think about building a machine that would take over the heart's work during the operation. The device would be located outside the body. And it would have to do the jobs of both the heart (pump the blood) and the lungs (add oxygen to the blood). The task seemed difficult but possible.

At exactly 8:05 A.M., Dr. Gibbon's thoughts were interrupted. The screen showed a sharp drop in Edith's blood pressure. No sooner had he sounded the alarm than the surgical team rushed into action. They sped through the steps of the operation: administering the anesthetic, opening the chest, opening the artery, removing the clot.

In seven minutes the operation was over. But seven minutes was too long. Edith had died.

In another sense, though, she lived on. Her struggle inspired Dr. Gibbon to spend the next twenty-three years building a machine that would save many lives.

THE OUTCOME

Dr. Gibbon received little encouragement from other doctors. Nevertheless he persevered, bringing the machine into being while continuing his career as a surgeon and a researcher. At long last, in 1935, he had a working model of a heart-lung machine.

The world's first operational heart-lung machine, designed by Dr. Gibbon in 1935.

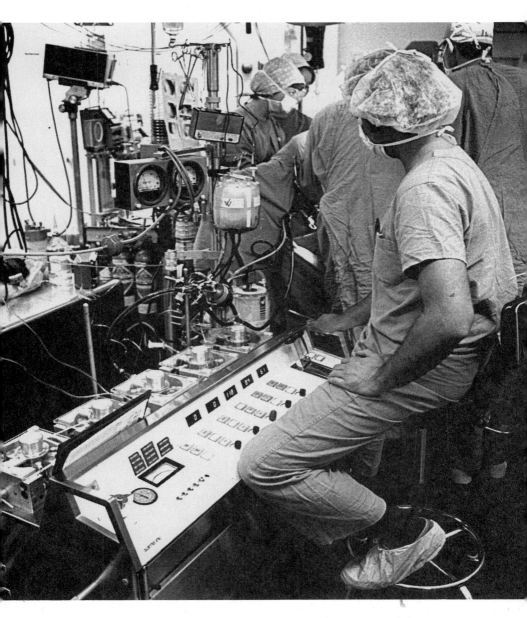

A modern heart-lung machine, performing its life-sustaining tasks during open-heart surgery

Dr. Gibbon decided to run the first test on a cat. He attached two tubes to the animal's heart. One carried blood from the heart to the machine, where it received a supply of oxygen to replace the carbon dioxide it contained. The other pumped the blood with the fresh oxygen back to the heart. The pump was built with enough power to send the blood circulating throughout the cat's body.

Next Dr. Gibbon clamped shut the cat's pulmonary artery. That should have killed the cat. But it didn't. The animal's circulation, breathing, and blood pressure stayed normal. For nearly four hours, Dr. Gibbon kept the cat hooked up to the heart-lung machine. It worked perfectly. The heart-lung machine had passed its first test.

Still, it was a big leap from a heart-lung machine that could keep a cat alive to one for human beings. For the next eighteen years Dr. Gibbon devoted all his time and energy to making every single part of the machine completely effective and reliable.

By 1953 the heart-lung machine was ready for human trials. On May 6 of that year, for the first time, Dr. Gibbon used the device in a human heart operation.

The patient was eighteen-year-old Cecilia Bavolek. The doctor connected Bavolek to the machine for forty-five minutes while surgeons repaired a defect in her heart. The results were excellent. The patient survived the surgery— and the time on the machine—with absolutely no ill effects.

Everyone considers the heart-lung machine the very first artificial heart. But it was, and still is, a huge, out-of-the-body piece of equipment that can only be used in an operating room. What about an artificial heart that could be placed *inside* the patient's body? Could such a device be built? And would it allow the patient to lead a normal, or at least close-to-normal, life?

5

TOWARD AN ARTIFICIAL

HEART IMPLANT

Tick-pfft, tick-pfft, tick-pfft, tick-pfft. The sound never stops in the basement of the Institute for Biomedical Engineering at the University of Utah Medical Center in Salt Lake City. It comes from a number of experimental artificial hearts being tested in tanks of water.

These artificial hearts pump away, day after day, year after year. They tell researchers how long they will run, what the weaknesses are, and how these weaknesses can be eliminated. The longest-running artificial heart in this lab has not missed a beat since 1978!

A few doors down the hall is an animal laboratory that contains several calves and sheep. These animals have had artificial heart implants. Their condition is being carefully studied to help design a better human artificial heart. One calf is remembered because it lived for nearly nine months with an artificial heart. The only reason it died was that the animal had grown too large for its original implant.

BASIC RESEARCH

The Institute for Biomedical Engineering is largely the brainchild of Dr. Willem Kolff. Born in Holland in 1911,

Dr. Kolff is the son of a physician. As a young doctor, Dr. Kolff lost a patient, a twenty-two-year-old man who suffered kidney failure. There was no known treatment for the condition at the time. But this experience of watching helplessly while the young man grew increasingly weak and finally died made a lasting impression on Dr. Kolff.

The loss led Dr. Kolff to think about the possibility of an artificial kidney, a device that could take over the kidney's job of removing waste products from the blood. Dr. Kolff set himself the task of trying to build such a device.

THE FIRST TESTS

By 1943 Dr. Kolff had a working model of an artificial kidney. It consisted of an enamel tank, a wooden rotating drum, 2 yards (1.8 m) of cellophane tubing, a small electric motor, and the water-pump seals from a Ford automobile.

The first human trials of the kidney were failures. All the patients died. It wasn't until 1946 that the machines saved the life of a sixty-seven-year-old woman. This success led to a new era in the use of artificial organs.

In 1950 Dr. Kolff emigrated to the United States and took a position at the famed Cleveland Clinic in Ohio. Here he applied his skills to improving the heart-lung machine. Seven years later he turned his attention to trying to develop an artificial heart. He made rapid progress and in 1957 did his first implantation of an artificial heart into a dog.

Dr. Kolff's dog lived for only an hour and a half. The doctor was very disappointed, but he found reason for optimism. If it worked that long, he reasoned, it could be made to perform for a much longer period. Dr. Kolff was soon back in his lab, working to create a better, more practical, artificial heart.

The University of Utah invited Dr. Kolff in 1967 to head a new Division of Artificial Organs. The first person that Dr. Kolff hired to work with him was William C.

Dr. Willem Kolff,
director of the
Institute for Biomedical
Engineering at the
University of Utah

DeVries (b. 1943), who was then a medical student at the University of Utah. Dr. DeVries was later to become the first surgeon to make a permanent implant of an artificial heart into a human being.

In time the Division of Artificial Organs was expanded to become the Institute for Biomedical Engineering. A major project of the institute was the development of an artificial heart. As the team that Dr. Kolff assembled prepared new, improved models, they tested them on animal subjects. Dr. Kolff and the others measured survival time not in days or months but in hours. One early big breakthrough was a sheep that lived fifty hours with an artificial heart.

ROUGH GOING

What Dr. Kolff wanted was to build an artificial heart that would be complete within the patient's chest. Finding a good source of power was his chief difficulty. First he thought of using electricity. When that didn't work out, he considered an artificial heart powered by nuclear energy. The device would be run by a miniature engine that got its power from the heat given off by a small bit of radioactive plutonium.

News of these nuclear experiments triggered a loud outcry from the scientific community and the public at large. Plutonium is one of the deadliest substances on earth. Its radiation can either kill or cause serious radiation sickness. And Dr. Kolff wanted to implant plutonium in people's bodies!

Government officials felt compelled to withdraw funding for the study. Research on a nuclear-powered artificial heart came to a halt.

However, a light went on in Dr. Kolff's mind. He realized that his difficulties mainly stemmed from his attempt to solve two giant problems at the same time. One was to build the mechanical pump. The other was to find an implantable source of power. He decided to concentrate on the pump and forget about the source of power for the time being.

All the artificial hearts he had built ran on compressed air. Why not get the compressed air from a machine outside the body? Then, after he had solved all the mechanical problems of the device itself, he would turn his full attention to finding a better source of power.

PERFECTING THE
ARTIFICIAL HEART

Dr. Kolff began to focus his energy on solving the problems with the existing mechanical devices. He constructed a model with a diaphragm, which is a flexible membrane of silicone rubber, inside a rigid hollow chamber. Pulses of compressed air raised the diaphragm. This squeezed the blood out of the chamber. In this way, the artificial heart moved the blood from chamber to chamber or into an artery. And mechanical valves controlled the flow, making sure that the blood moved in the right direction.

As time went on, Dr. Kolff and his team improved the mechanical features of the device. They also became more skilled in their surgical techniques. The survival rates for their laboratory animals continued to rise—twelve days, eighteen days, and finally, a month.

In 1971 Dr. Kolff hired Robert K. Jarvik (b. 1946) for $100 a week to serve as an assistant design engineer. While still in high school, Jarvik, the son of a surgeon, had invented a device to staple tissue together during surgery instead of relying on hand suturing. While working for Dr. Kolff, Jarvik also earned his medical degree.

Jarvik immediately got to work on Kolff's model of the artificial heart. He was highly motivated to succeed. His own father had nearly died of heart disease seven years earlier. "I decided I better do something about this," he later recalled.

Jarvik's first improvement on the artificial heart was to make it smaller and more efficient. He also designed a new diaphragm of smooth polyurethane to replace the one of silicone rubber. By 1984, Jarvik's hearts were keeping calves alive for as long as three months.

Meanwhile, the same team was devising new and better procedures to prepare the patient for the artificial heart implant. They tested ways to leave more of the upper part of the heart intact, with its connected arteries and veins. These parts of the heart were seldom diseased. Having them in place made the artificial heart simpler to build and easier to attach. The artificial heart became mostly the two ventricles.

The researchers also experimented with drugs to prevent the blood from coagulating, or clotting. These lumps in the blood could block a blood vessel and kill the patient by interfering with the blood flow.

Dr. Robert K. Jarvik, designer of the Jarvik-7
artificial heart, is seen here with a calf that
lived for 268 days with an artificial heart.

OTHER ARTIFICIAL HEARTS

Drs. Kolff, Jarvik, and DeVries were not the only ones working to develop an artificial heart. Teams at two other major medical centers—Baylor-Rice Artificial Heart Program in Houston, Texas, led by Dr. Michael E. DeBakey, and the Pennsylvania State University Division of Artificial Hearts at the Hershey Medical Center in Hershey, Pennsylvania, under Dr. William S. Pierce—as well as others—were far along in their efforts to develop an artificial heart.

These researchers had solved, in similar ways, the three major problems in creating a practical artificial heart:

1. The engineering problem: to build a device that does the job efficiently, safely, and reliably.
2. The surgical problem: to implant the device without causing further damage to an already seriously ill patient.
3. The medical problem: to sustain the patient after the implantation by controlling the infection and clotting dangers.

They also went through a host of experimental animal implantations, both to expose weaknesses in the device and to prepare and train the team for human implantation.

On April 4, 1969, Dr. Denton A. Cooley (b. 1920) implanted the heart developed at the Baylor-Rice Artificial Heart Program into a human patient. The heart was used as a temporary replacement for one that was about to fail. Dr. Cooley merely hoped to keep the patient alive long enough to find a human heart for transplantation. The Baylor-Rice artificial heart did indeed work well for three days until it was replaced by a donor heart.

RUSH TO IMPLANT

Throughout this period, everyone at the Institute for Biomedical Engineering continued working, getting closer and closer to a permanent artificial heart implant. As word got out, reporters began calling Dr. Kolff and asking when he would be ready. His reply was always the same: "I will be disappointed if the artificial heart is not ready in three years, and three years ago I said the same thing."

Jarvik and the others had made a lot of progress. They had whittled the large artificial heart used in the calf experiments down to a size that would fit in a human chest. The new, superior model that resulted is called the Jarvik-7.

Slightly bigger than a human heart, the Jarvik-7 heart weighs the same, 10 ounces (280 g). It consists of two hollow chambers made of the plastic polyurethane on an aluminum base. These chambers correspond to the left and right ventricles of the human heart.

Stretched across the bottom of each chamber is the thin, polyurethane diaphragm. Two 6-foot-long (1.8-m) plastic tubes are attached to the bottoms of the chambers. They leave the body through two holes in the person's abdomen, just beneath the rib cage.

The two flexible tubes go to a large, 375-pound (170-kg) air compressor, called the heart driver. This unit, with all the backup equipment, is big and bulky and is kept on a cart with wheels. The doctors call the unit the "shopping cart." The heart driver must always be at the patient's side.

Pulses of air go through the tubes to the two chambers. The air pressure pushes up the diaphragms, forcing the blood out through the pulmonary artery or the aorta. In between the puffs of air the diaphragm collapses and the chambers fill with blood.

Dr. Jack Kolff, son of Dr. Willem Kolff and a heart surgeon himself, contributed valuable information on surgical techniques for artificial heart implantation. He worked out a way to properly position the heart in the chest. He even implanted the artificial heart in some patients who had just died and found that he could maintain their blood circulation, even though they were legally dead.

After graduating from medical school and taking his training in surgery elsewhere, Dr. DeVries returned as a

The Jarvik-7 artificial heart

surgeon to the University of Utah Medical Center in 1980. He also rejoined Dr. Kolff's Institute for Biomedical Engineering. His intent was to prepare himself to implant an artificial heart in a human patient. In addition to his heavy schedule of heart operations, Dr. DeVries saved one day a week to work with the artificial heart as a way of further sharpening his skills. He estimates that he put artificial hearts in about two hundred animals and twenty cadavers.

Everything was finally ready. Dr. Kolff's team, drawing on their own research as well as on the research done at other medical centers, believed they had developed a working, reliable artificial heart to be a permanent replacement for a diseased human heart. The doctors working with Dr. Kolff knew how to remove the diseased heart and which drugs would prevent the formation of blood clots and infections. With the heart driver they had a source of power

[51]

to run the mechanical heart. It was big and cumbersome, but it could be depended on to do the job. And they had a surgeon who had been practicing and refining his technique in preparation for the first permanent human artificial heart implant.

In June 1980, Dr. DeVries applied to the University of Utah Institutional Review Board, the committee that had to give permission for him to implant the Jarvik-7 in a human patient. Permission was granted. The federal government's Food and Drug Administration (FDA) gave its approval, too. But the FDA insisted that it could only be implanted in a patient who could not be taken off the heart-lung machine after open-heart surgery.

For nine months Dr. DeVries and the Utah team sought such a patient in vain. They were finally told they could look instead for what is called a "Class IV" patient. This is a category that is made up of heart patients who are suffering from very serious heart disease, who cannot be treated in any other way, and who show symptoms even while resting in bed. Also, the candidate had to be over eighteen years of age and not be eligible for a heart transplant.

Over twenty potential patients were screened by Dr. DeVries and a committee that included two cardiologists, a psychiatrist, a social worker, a nurse, and a representative from the University of Utah. Some patients were too sick; they had almost no chance of surviving. Some weren't sick enough; they might live for months or years without the implant. Some were acceptable physically but were not stable enough psychologically. A three-year-old girl was refused because she was too young. One man, who was turned down, threatened to lie on the hospital steps until he died. But the search went on.

Finally, in 1982, Barney Clark was selected and a Jarvik-7 model was placed in his chest. The era of permanent artificial heart implants had begun.

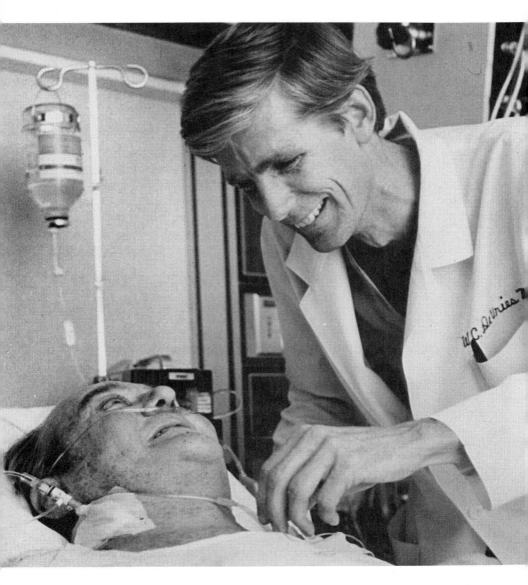

Dr. William C. DeVries with Barney Clark, the world's first recipient of a permanent artificial heart

Over the following years, patients with permanent Jarvik-7 implants suffered such postoperative complications as strokes, internal bleeding, breathing difficulty, and infection. The doctors suspected two possible causes. One is that blood clots form in the device itself. The clots then break free and move through the bloodstream to a place where they actually block a blood vessel. Another is that the artificial heart may sometimes be pumping too hard for the recipient's weakened circulatory system. The increased blood flow may then cause additional damage.

Meanwhile, researchers on the Pennsylvania State University team continued to improve their Penn State heart. They wanted to correct some of the problems that were arising with the Jarvik-7 heart.

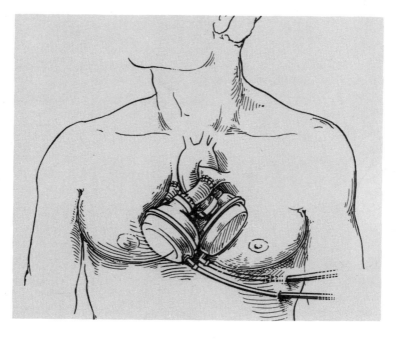

The Penn State artificial heart

Basically, the Penn State heart is the same as the Jarvik-7. It consists of two hollow, rigid chambers with soft diaphragms that expand and contract to pump the blood. But the inner linings of the chambers are absolutely smooth and without any seams. This is to avoid the tendency of blood to coagulate on any irregularity over which it flows. Also, the Penn State heart automatically adjusts to the patient's need for more or less blood flow. When the patient is active, it pumps more blood.

The first implantation of the Penn State heart took place on October 18, 1985, with Dr. William S. Pierce as the surgeon in charge. It was planned to serve as a bridge to a human heart transplant. The artificial heart functioned without problem for the ten days it took to locate a human heart for transplant.

RESEARCH TODAY

Almost all centers of artificial heart research are now trying to eliminate the need for the outside heart driver. They are doing experiments on a totally self-contained electrical artificial heart. The patient would wear a portable electric power pack of long-life batteries around the waist or on the shoulder. Some models would deliver the power through a thin wire that would lead in, through the skin, to the artificial heart. A more advanced version would send the electricity through the skin, without requiring an opening in the skin at all. The researchers hope that this new device will be a permanent replacement for a diseased heart. It has already kept a calf alive for over seven months.

According to the best estimates it will be 1990 before the electrical artificial heart will be ready for human use. By then, according to Dr. Pierce, today's artificial hearts will "seem to us like the Model T Ford."

Perhaps Dr. Kolff best stated the goal of today's researchers: "We do not want just to prolong life, but to create happiness."

6

BARNEY CLARK AND

PERMANENT IMPLANTS

Barney Clark was his name. He was born on January 21, 1921, in Provo, Utah. When Barney was only twelve years old his father died and the young boy had to support his mother. At first he sold hot dogs at the local ballpark. Later he mowed lawns, babysat, and worked in a grocery store. Besides these afterschool jobs, Barney, who grew to be a big 6 feet, 3 inches (1.9 m) tall, found time to play on his high school football team.

Barney Clark paid the tuition for college and dental school out of the wages he earned for his part-time work. In 1944 he married his childhood sweetheart, Una Loy, and they had three children, two boys and a girl. He opened his own dental office in Des Moines, Washington, a suburb of Seattle, and soon built up a busy, successful practice. When not busy with his patients or his family, Clark was playing golf. It was about then that he started his two-pack-a-day smoking habit.

In 1977 Clark retired from dentistry. Money was no problem; he had enough saved for all his needs. And he seemed to be in good health, fully able to enjoy all the pleasures of his retirement. But then, scarcely one year later, he began to notice some breathing difficulties and a general tiredness. Even getting around the golf course was difficult. Clark knew that something was wrong.

THE DIAGNOSIS

The doctors first thought that Clark's problem was in his lungs. More careful examination, though, revealed serious heart disease. The disease is called cardiomyopathy, a sickness of unknown cause that destroys the heart muscles.

The cardiomyopathy was making Clark's heart muscles more and more flabby. They were not strong enough to pump the blood around his body. As a result, his lungs and other organs and tissue were filling up with fluid. This robbed Clark of his strength and made it hard for him to breathe. The doctors held out little hope. There is no cure for cardiomyopathy. It is nearly always fatal.

Still, the doctors did not give up. They tried powerful drugs that expanded the blood vessels and made it easier for the heart to pump. The drugs helped for a while, but then Clark's condition began to slip again. The doctors suggested a new experimental drug that was supposed to make the heart muscles work harder. A slight improvement was followed by a return of the disease to its deadly course.

In October 1982, Clark's doctors suggested that he visit the University of Utah Medical Center. They proposed that he consider becoming a candidate for the artificial heart researchers were developing there. Clark went, learned about the procedure, and discussed the risks and possible benefits. The visit included a trip to the laboratory where animals were being kept alive by implanted artificial hearts. The doctors working on the heart told him they felt ready to try the heart on a human patient.

Barney Clark was not impressed. The idea of being tied forever to an outside source of power for the artificial heart did not appeal to him. Jokingly he said that he would not mind being the hundredth recipient of an artificial heart, but he was not too sure about being the first.

By November 1982, Barney Clark was bedridden. Sinking fast, he knew that his heart was almost useless and that he was close to death. His thoughts kept going back to the artificial heart in Utah. Someone had to be the first volunteer for an implant. Should he submit, even though he had little faith in the device? Did he have a better alternative?

The days went on. His condition worsened. Over Thanksgiving he grew critically ill. On Saturday, November 27, he telephoned Dr. William C. DeVries, the chief surgeon on the artificial heart team. Clark uttered two words, "It's time." Dr. DeVries understood.

On Monday, November 29, Barney Clark flew from Seattle to Salt Lake City. A waiting helicopter whisked him to the University of Utah hospital. Barney Clark was about to become the central figure in one of the most dramatic and historic events in the entire history of medicine—the first permanent implantation of an artificial heart into a human being!

APPROACHING IMPLANT

Clark was admitted into the medical center immediately. A round of examinations, tests, and interviews began. Before proceeding the doctors made sure that no other medical or surgical treatment offered Clark any hope of a cure, or at least control over, his condition. Also, they convinced themselves that Clark was not so ill that the procedure was doomed to fail. Dr. DeVries was in favor of the artificial heart implant. He said of Clark, "He was too old for a transplant, there were no drugs that could help; the only thing he could look forward to was dying."

Members of a University of Utah committee made up of physicians, psychiatrists, social workers, and administrators spoke to Clark. They questioned and tested him to determine his mental and psychological state.

Margaret Miller, a social worker on the committee, summed up their findings: "He had a very strong will to live, had an intelligent, thorough understanding of his disease and his options, was a flexible person who could make compromises and had a loving, supportive family. This man had all those things in abundance." She added, "This man was worth waiting for."

Clark was asked to read and sign an eleven-page informed consent form. The form spelled out all the dangers of implanting an artificial heart. The patient put his name on the form on the day he arrived. His signature was firm and steady.

The following day, they gave him the same papers to sign again, just in case he had second thoughts. But this time his name on the paper was faint and shaky. It was not that Clark was in doubt. It was because his heart was failing so rapidly.

The surgery was scheduled to take place 8:00 A.M. on the morning of Thursday, December 2. But on the preceding afternoon, Clark's condition took a sudden turn for the worse. His heartbeat, which had been weak and irregular, became very rapid and even more feeble. The heart was failing. Clark's skin was turning blue, and fluid was collecting in his vital organs.

MAKING MEDICAL HISTORY

By Wednesday evening, Dr. DeVries decided that the operation could not wait. Clark was rushed to the operating room and immediately anesthetized—without even receiving the standard preoperation medication. At exactly 11:27 P.M., Dr. DeVries, assisted by a team of fourteen surgeons, cardiologists, nurses, and medical technicians, began the procedure. Dr. Jarvik stood by as an observer. He was prepared to help if there was any difficulty with the device itself.

As Ravel's *Bolero* played softly in the background. Dr. DeVries made an 18-inch (46-cm) cut in Clark's chest to expose his heart. The watching doctors were shocked at what they saw. Clark's heart was about twice the normal size and so soft and flabby that they were afraid that it would stop at any moment. The highly trained surgical team quickly hooked Clark up to the heart-lung machine. Now, at last, they knew that he would not expire right away. The first crisis was past.

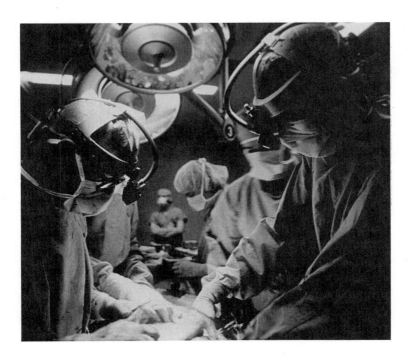

The operation of Barney Clark
gets underway.

Working carefully and deftly, Dr. DeVries cut away the badly diseased left and right ventricles. Once they were gone, Barney Clark had no heart. Without the implant he was doomed. There was no turning back. "It was almost a spiritual experience for everyone in the room," commented Dr. DeVries.

Dr. DeVries had to sew Dacron cuffs, or fittings, to the right and left atria, which had been left in Clark's body. He also had to attach similar cuffs to the aorta and pulmonary arteries. The artificial heart would be attached to these cuffs.

In a healthy heart this step would offer no difficulty. But Clark's heart was very unhealthy. The disease and the drugs he had been taking had made the walls of the atria and arteries weak and paper thin. It took about two hours to attach the cuffs and make sure that they would not leak. The second crisis had been overcome.

A nurse then reached over to the surgeon and handed him a small package, the size of a woman's purse. It was covered with a pale-blue sterile cloth that was held closed by two strips of tape. On one tape was written "Total Artificial Heart No. 1." Inside was the Jarvik-7 artificial heart.

Dr. DeVries snapped the artificial heart into place on the cuffs. He ran two clear plastic tubes from the two chambers of the artificial heart to the heart driver through small openings he had made in Clark's abdomen. But when Dr. DeVries turned on the power, the left ventricle did not pump properly.

Twice the surgeon took out the artificial heart, checked all the connections, and put it back in place. Still the pressure remained far below normal. Finally, Dr. DeVries removed the separate left ventricle and replaced it with a spare, backup unit. The new one worked perfectly, and the third crisis had been resolved.

The artificial heart was now doing as well as had been expected. Dr. DeVries proceeded step-by-step through the

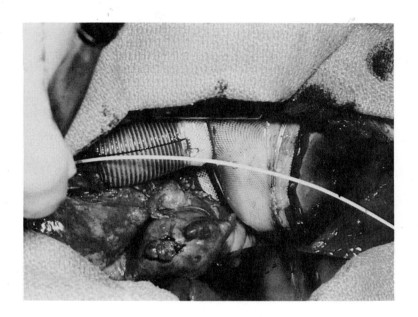

*This photograph shows the actual implant
of the device in Clark's chest.*

rest of the operation just as he had practiced many times before. Soon after 4:00 A.M. Clark was taken off the heart-lung machine. His life now depended completely on the Jarvik-7 heart that clicked away in his chest without missing a beat.

At 7:05 A.M. Clark was wheeled out of the operating room and into a special intensive care room. The operation had lasted seven-and-a-half hours. By coincidence, it had come exactly fifteen years, less one day, after Dr. Barnard's first heart transplant operation.

FOLLOWING SURGERY

The doctors and nurses kept their eyes on Clark and on the monitors that were tracking his condition. His pulse and blood pressure were better than they had been for years. The fluids were draining out of his lungs and abdomen. Gradually his skin color changed from a sickly blue to a healthy pink.

That afternoon Clark came out of the anesthesia. Wide awake and alert, he nodded to the doctors to let them know that he was not in pain. The very modest Dr. DeVries said, "I think it's been a success."

The first sign of trouble came on Saturday afternoon, just over forty-eight hours after the operation. Clark experienced some pain in his lungs and had difficulty in breathing. An examination revealed the cause of the distress. Some bubbles of air had worked their way into his chest wall.

Returning Clark to the operating room, Dr. DeVries opened the patient's chest again. He saw the cause of the problem. Air was escaping out of a number of small holes in Clark's lungs and getting into the chest wall. Dr. DeVries stitched the holes closed and inserted a drain to remove any air that might collect in the future.

Two days of improvement were followed by another setback. Clark was chatting with Dr. DeVries early on Tuesday morning. "How am I doing?" Clark asked. Barely had Dr. DeVries replied, "Just fine," when Clark went into violent convulsions. His whole body trembled. Within moments Dr. DeVries had Clark connected to a respirator and had injected him with drugs to control the convulsions.

Despite the immediate medical attention, it was nearly three hours before Clark stopped shaking. The cause was thought to be an excess of pressure on the blood vessels in the brain. The artificial heart was working *too* well for Clark's weak body.

As a result of this episode, Clark did not seem as sharp as before. Perfectly alert and rational at times, he appeared confused on some other occasions. The doctors were not sure of the cause. It might be some brain damage or the

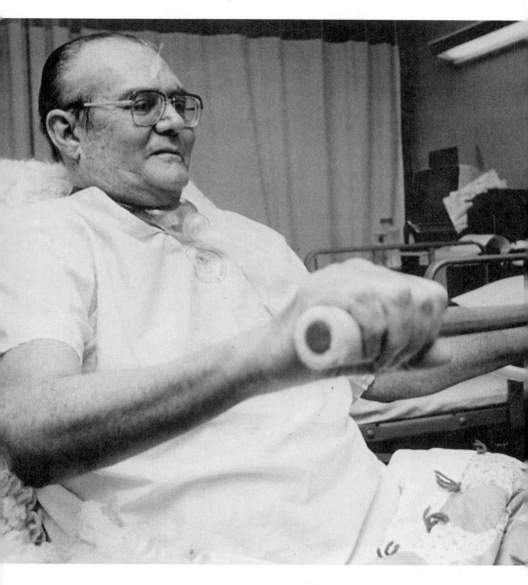

Barney Clark after his seemingly successful
operation, lifting himself out of bed

emotional strain and depression that almost always follows major heart surgery.

The morning of December 14 brought another turn of events. Clark's blood pressure plummeted despite the fact that the drive system of the artificial heart was working perfectly. The problem had to be in the artificial heart itself. Back to the operating room. On opening Clark's chest for the third time, they found that the valve in the left ventricle had broken. For the second time they replaced the entire left ventricle.

Still again Clark bounced back. As the days passed he was able to sit up, stand up, and even take a few steps. By Christmas he was joking with the nurses and eating his first solid food. But then he began having severe nosebleeds, which the doctors were only able to control with further surgery.

Throughout, Clark kept up his spirits. In a television interview on March 21 he spoke about the artificial heart implant for people with terminal heart disease: "It's worth it if the alternative is that they either die or they have it done."

The very next day, though, Clark ran into new and worse complications. He began to suffer attacks of nausea and vomiting. The vomiting irritated his lungs. He developed pneumonia. This was followed by periods of high fever and a bad infection in his colon. His kidneys failed next. And at 10:02 P.M. on March 23, 1983, after nearly four months of living with an artificial heart that beat nearly 13 million times, Barney Clark succumbed. Drs. DeVries and Jarvik were at his bedside.

The cause of death was the failure of the kidneys and other organs. The artificial heart kept clicking away. A hospital worker actually had to shut it off.

WILLIAM J. SCHROEDER

Bull Schroeder was what they called him at the military munitions plant at which he worked in Crane, Indiana. A father of six and a longtime smoker he was big—6 feet (1.8 m), 200 pounds (91 kg)—tough, and stubborn. Yet, soon after his fiftieth birthday Schroeder suffered a severe heart attack. His doctors suggested a double coronary by-pass operation. In 1983 they grafted two veins from his leg into his chest to replace the coronary arteries that were blocked by fatty deposits.

Unfortunately, the surgery did not help for very long. Schroeder grew weaker and weaker. In May 1984 he had to leave his job. By around November he could hardly walk and often woke up at night gasping for breath. His doctors suggested he see Dr. DeVries about an artificial heart im-plant.

Dr. DeVries was then at the Humana Heart Institute International at the Humana Hospital-Audubon in Louis-ville, Kentucky. He had left the University of Utah Medical Center in August 1984. Many people were shocked to learn of his move. The University of Utah is a nonprofit in-stitution, while Humana Hospital is part of a profit-making chain of nearly a hundred hospitals in the United States and Europe.

Dr. DeVries, it seems, had been frustrated in his at-tempts to do the work he wanted in Utah. Every implant required prior approval from the university's Institutional Review Board. For various reasons they had asked him to delay a second implant after Barney Clark. And then, when they finally gave permission, it was for only one implant, which troubled Dr. DeVries. "I don't like to see people die while I wait for the red tape," he said.

Humana Hospital, he hoped, would give him the free-dom he sought. "My view is that I have been able to set up this project exactly the way I wanted to, and there has been no question about what devices cost." As part of the arrangement that brought Dr. DeVries to Louisville, Hu-mana agreed to bear the cost of a hundred artificial heart implants.

Dr. DeVries examined Schroeder at the Humana Hos-pital. Schroeder was suffering from cardiomyopathy, just

[67]

like Barney Clark. His heart was barely beating. Dr. DeVries guessed that he would not survive for more than a few days. At fifty-two-years old, Schroeder was over the age limit for a human heart transplant. The doctor decided an artificial heart implant was in order.

On the evening of November 24, 1984, a priest gave Schroeder the last rites of the Catholic church. And the next morning he was wheeled into surgery for the second permanent artificial heart implant. The heart was a slightly improved version of the Jarvik-7 that Dr. DeVries had implanted in Barney Clark almost two years earlier.

William Schroeder was in much better shape than Clark. First, he was younger and less disabled before the surgery. Second, doctors had learned a great deal from treating Clark that they could then apply to help Schroeder.

Schroeder recovered very quickly. Within a few weeks he was able to speak with President Reagan on the telephone, make jokes with the doctors, and even drink a can of beer while being televised. The doctors had a new, miniature air compressor ready to use when Schroeder would be able to walk. The 11-pound (5-kg), battery-powered pack could be carried on a shoulder strap to give the patient complete mobility. Although Schroeder was briefly connected to this new unit, he was never strong enough to walk with it.

On the morning of December 13, Schroeder went on a wheelchair tour of the hospital, the big air compressor machine wheeling alongside. That afternoon he had another television interview. There was every reason to believe that he was well on his way to a complete recovery.

But disaster struck that evening while he was having dinner with his wife, Margaret. Suddenly his eyes rolled up in his head and he froze in position. The doctors rushed into Schroeder's room. They recognized the symptoms. He had suffered a stroke.

The probable cause was a blood clot that had gone to his brain. When blood flows over a foreign substance it

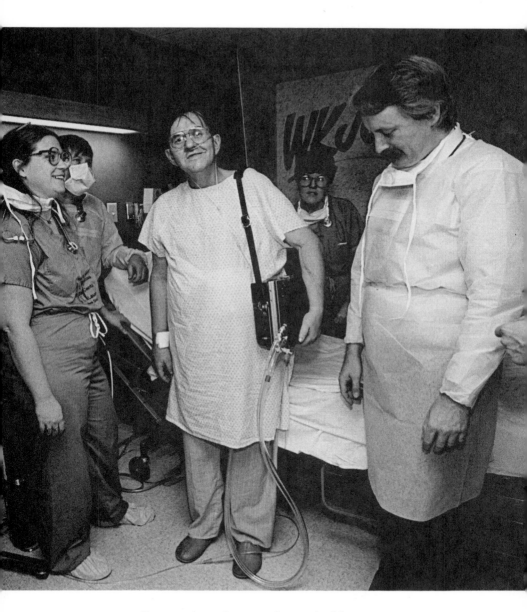

*William Schroeder stands up, holding onto
the battery-operated power supply*

tends to form clots. The likelihood was that a clot had formed in the artificial heart and been carried to his brain, where it blocked a blood vessel, leading to the stroke.

Dr. DeVries treated Schroeder with blood thinners to break up the clot and restore normal circulation. But damage had been done. Schroeder lost some of his memory, his coordination, his speech, and his very special personality.

Other setbacks occurred over the following months. Schroeder had some seizures that the doctors thought might be small strokes. A mysterious fever that spiked up to 105°F (41°C) left him without appetite, dull and sluggish in movement, and barely able to speak at all.

In the spring of 1985, Schroeder's condition grew somewhat better. He felt stronger and could speak in short sentences. With his wife, Margaret, he moved to an apartment across the street from Humana Hospital. The apartment was specially equipped with emergency alarms and an intercom connected to the hospital so that he could get help at a moment's notice. A third stroke, though, forced Schroeder to return to the hospital. And a final stroke and lung infection in August 1986 led to his death.

It had been far from a good life either for Schroeder or his wife during the months he was living with the artificial heart. As Margaret said while he was still alive, "At first I thought it was just for Bill so he would be able to get better and come home. And now I see it as more of a research experiment. The longer he lives the more information they get. Only for us it's just hard sometimes."

At the time of this writing, five people have received permanent artificial heart implants. Four were done by Dr. DeVries and one by Dr. Bjarne Semb in Sweden, with Dr. DeVries assisting. Three of the patients died after relatively short periods. Murray Haydon lived for sixteen months. Schroeder survived longest, living for 620 days, close to two years.

7
BRIDGE
TO TRANSPLANT

"Someone, somewhere, please hear my plea. A plea for a heart for my husband. I see him lying there, breathing and knowing that within his chest is a man-made implement where there should be a God-given heart."

This was the urgent appeal that Mrs. Haskell Karp made on television and in the newspapers early in April 1969. Over the previous ten years her husband had suffered a series of major heart attacks. On March 5 the desperately sick forty-seven-year-old man was admitted to the Texas Heart Institute at St. Luke's Episcopal Hospital in Houston, Texas.

According to Dr. Denton A. Cooley, a leading heart surgeon at St. Luke's, Karp was suffering from advanced coronary artery disease and heart block. Many of the arteries supplying blood to his heart were fully or mostly clogged.

For a month Dr. Cooley and the other doctors treated Karp with various drugs. There was no improvement. Dr. Cooley spoke to Karp about surgery. The patient did not want a human heart transplant. But he was in favor of an operation to try to repair his heart surgically.

The operation was set for April 4. When Dr. Cooley exposed Karp's heart he found that most of the heart muscle had been destroyed. About two-thirds of the left ventricle and almost all of the septum had been replaced by scar tissue. The surgeon tried to repair the badly damaged heart but was unsuccessful.

No donor heart was available for transplant. Dr. Cooley felt he had only two choices: either watch Karp die on the operating table or implant an artificial heart. The only artificial heart available at that time had been developed by Dr. Domingo Liotta and Dr. Michael E. DeBakey at the Artificial Heart Program of Baylor and Rice universities in Houston. Dr. Cooley implanted the artificial heart as a temporary, emergency measure. Many years later the use of an artificial heart to keep a patient alive while waiting for a human heart came to be called a "bridge to transplant."

THE FIRST
TEMPORARY IMPLANT

Karp was conscious fifteen minutes after the operation. He was able to respond to commands and move his arms and legs. Meanwhile, a search started for a donor heart. That was when Mrs. Karp made her touching plea.

A telephone call came to Houston from Lawrence, Massachusetts. It brought welcome news of a donor. Mrs. Barbara Ewan, thirty-nine, had been in a coma at Lawrence General Hospital since March 19. On April 5 the oxygen supply to her brain failed and she was pronounced brain dead, even though her heart continued to beat. The woman's family and physician agreed to donate her heart to Karp.

After its arrival at St. Luke's in Houston on April 7, the heart of Mrs. Ewan was put into Karp's chest in place of the artificial heart. The artificial heart had given the

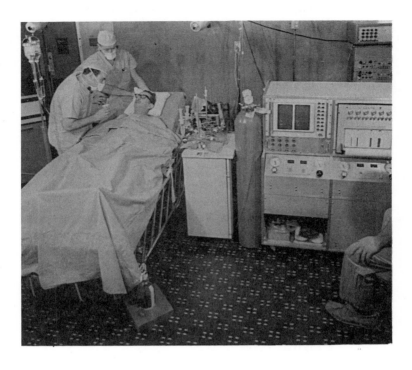

*Haskell Karp, the world's first recipient
of an artificial heart. The device was
used as a bridge to transplant, not as a
permanent replacement for his heart. However,
Karp died of kidney failure and pneumonia
soon after his transplant operation.*

doctors the time they needed to find and transplant a human heart.

A few hours after the operation, though, Karp began to show signs of pneumonia. Although the doctors treated it as best they could, his condition grew worse. And on April 8, after sixty-four hours on the artificial heart and thirty-two hours with the human transplant, Karp died.

A RISKY BUSINESS

The artificial heart that Karp received in 1969 was never intended for permanent implantation. But aside from two emergency temporary implantations, all the following implants were of devices designed to run indefinitely. Barney Clark in 1982, William Schroeder in 1984, and Murray Haydon, Leif Stenberg, and Jack Burcham in 1985 all received permanent Jarvik-7 artificial hearts.

Permanent implants have produced mixed results. Schroeder survived longest, living nearly twenty-one months with his artificial heart. But even he suffered while he was alive with serious, lasting damage from his strokes. The others lived from a minimum of ten days to a maximum of sixteen months. All developed complications that affected them physically or mentally.

By the fall of 1985, the thinking of the medical profession swung back to the temporary use of artificial hearts. A conference on heart transplantation and implantation was held in Washington, D.C., in October of that year. Many of the leading heart surgeons were present. They concluded that the artificial heart, in its present state, was an extremely crude and risky long-term treatment for heart disease.

Citing the ever-improving success of human heart transplants, Dr. DeVries said, "There is no question that if you have a choice you have a transplant." But given the limited number of available donor hearts it is foolhardy to depend on that source alone. Therefore, the doctors suggested, artificial heart research should continue. For now, though, they should only be used as a bridge to sustain very sick patients until a human heart transplant can be done.

IMPORTANT MILESTONES

While the Washington conference was going on, Michael Drummond, age twenty-five, was at the University of Arizona Medical Center in Tucson, Arizona. He was to become the youngest recipient of an artificial heart. A severe viral infection had attacked the muscles of Drummond's heart. In August his doctors sent him to the University of Arizona Medical Center for a heart transplant.

When Drummond arrived at the medical center he was near death. No donor heart was available. The doctors could not just stand by and let this young man die before their eyes. And so, on August 29, 1985, they implanted a Jarvik-7 artificial heart to keep him alive while awaiting a human heart.

For nine days, the artificial heart kept Drummond in stable condition. Then, when nineteen-year-old Tarro Griffin was killed in a motorcycle accident in Texas, Griffin's heart was flown to Arizona. On September 7, it was transplanted into Drummond as a replacement for the Jarvik unit.

Drummond's recovery was so speedy that on November 14 he was released from the hospital. This gave Drummond his second claim to fame. He became the first person to have an artificial heart implanted as a bridge to a successful heart transplant.

Another milestone in the bridge-to-transplant saga came on December 19, 1985. That day, forty-year-old Mary Lund became the first woman to receive an artificial heart. The heart to be implanted was a Jarvik-7. It was intended to stabilize her condition while she awaited a transplant.

The original Jarvik-7, however, would not fit in her chest. It was built for adult males. A slightly smaller model was substituted. The surgery was performed at the Minneapolis Heart Institute at Abbott Northwestern Hospital in Minnesota. The surgeon in charge, Dr. Lyle Joyce, had been part of the original team that had implanted the first artificial heart in Barney Clark in 1982.

Forty-three days after Mary Lund's artificial heart implant, a donor heart was found. Mrs. Lund received the transplant on January 31, 1986. Although she was never

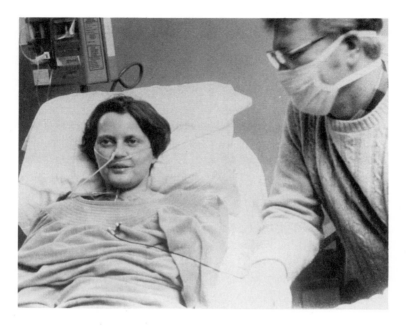

Mary Lund, the world's first female recipient of an artificial heart

formally released from the hospital, she was able to spend some weekends at home. But in October her condition grew worse and she died on October 14, 1986, of kidney failure.

To date there have been seventeen bridge-to-transplant operations. Only two of the patients have died. Using the artificial heart as a bridge to transplant seems to hold great promise for some of those suffering with severe heart disease.

DIFFICULT ISSUES

Bridge to transplant raises some thorny problems, however. "We have in this country more than sixty heart-transplant centers," said Dr. Shumway of the Stanford University Medical Center, "and everyone has a waiting list of people who are just about dead. If you put someone on the artificial heart all you do is put him at the top of the priority list." Dr. Shumway insists that the procedure will not save additional lives. It will only save *different* lives.

Imagine a situation where two patients are awaiting a transplant. Patient A is an excellent candidate. He could probably lead a normal life with a transplanted heart. Patient B is desperately ill. He might not survive, even with a transplant. Since patient B is so near death he is given the artificial heart as a bridge.

Then a single donor heart is found. The temptation is to give the human heart to patient B, who has the bridge-to-transplant heart. This denies the transplant to patient A, who is a better candidate for a human transplant.

Supporters of bridge-to-transplant surgery disagree. They say that temporary implantation is worthwhile and should be continued as long as it saves lives.

A bridge implant is like a double-edged sword. It improves the chances for survival, since it saves patients who might die while waiting for a donor heart. But at the same time, it decreases the likelihood of survival. The twin operations, implantation and then transplantation, tax the strength of patients who are already very sick.

Bridge to transplant is a new procedure. Doctors in several medical and research centers are working to learn more about how and when to do these two-part operations. They are also carefully following the patients' conditions after heart implant and transplant.

At the same time, there is growing concern about the ethical, psychological, and legal questions of heart transplants and implants. We will look at some of these questions in the following chapters. Experts in various fields are shedding new light every day on the complex and highly controversial issues that surround the artificial heart discussion.

8

ETHICAL ISSUES

Haskell Karp received the very first temporary artificial heart implant, in 1969. But neither the people who were developing the artificial heart, the hospital, nor any government agency had given permission for the implantation. Dr. Denton A. Cooley, the surgeon, justified his actions by saying that he wanted to do everything medically or surgically possible to save his patient's life.

Thus, the first human implantation of an artificial heart raised some important ethical questions: How far should a physician go in trying to keep a patient alive? Does the imminent death of a patient justify the doctor's taking actions that hold so little hope of success? When, if ever, should a physician stop trying to save a dying patient? To what extent should the doctor consider the patient's future quality of life?

Just before Jack Burcham was fitted with an artificial heart on April 14, 1985, doctors estimated he had two months to live. Right after the operation, Burcham's condition took a turn for the worse. Ten days later he was dead. Far from extending his life, the artificial heart probably cut it short.

Other ethical issues occur here. Who should receive the

hearts—those close to death or those with some time to live? Is the implant of an artificial heart experimental or therapeutic?

PATIENT SELECTION AND HUMAN EXPERIMENTATION

Two heart patients are admitted to the hospital with failing hearts. One used to smoke heavily, eat rich and fattening foods, and never exercised. The other took good care of his health but was struck suddenly by a deadly virus that was destroying the muscles of his heart. The doctors have only one donor heart available. Who should get it?

Several patients are under the care of the same heart surgeon. One is seriously ill and will probably not survive transplantation or implantation. The others have a good chance of making complete recoveries with a new heart. The family of the first patient launches a nationwide publicity campaign. On television and radio and in newspapers his wife and children beg and plead for a donor heart. The publicity gets results and a heart is flown to the hospital. Who should get it?

Three men are in the intensive care unit of a large hospital. All are suffering with cardiomyopathy. The youngest is twenty-five-years-old. The middle-aged one is forty-nine. And the third has just passed his fifty-fifth birthday. Only one heart is on hand. Who should get it?

Mrs. A. and Mr. B. are both in need of heart transplants. The woman supports her invalid husband and three children. Mr. B. is an unemployed drifter, without any family or close friends. Again, there is only one heart. Who should get it?

There are two heart patients in the same city. Their condition is about the same. One is being treated by a world-famous cardiologist at the biggest and best-equipped medical center. The other is under the care of a young staff doctor in an inner-city hospital. Which patient should get the first heart that becomes available?

These are some typical cases. Each one presents a different ethical dilemma for the doctors who must make selections for heart implants and transplants.

With advances in transplantation and implantation technology, situations like these have been developing with increasing frequency. There is a great need to set standards for patient selection and for experimentation on human subjects. Experts in medical ethics are now trying to work out fair and moral positions on the relative importance of such factors as social worth, age, family responsibilities, wealth, and so on. They have made some progress. But much remains to be done.

In the early 1960s, the Food and Drug Administration (FDA) and the U.S. Public Health Service–National Institutes of Health developed a set of ethical guidelines for human experimentation. Included was a new requirement. Before any research on humans would be funded by the federal government, there had to be a review of the proposal by a panel of doctors and scientists.

Dr. Cooley was criticized for not consulting the government or the medical panel before he operated on Haskell Karp. This was despite the fact that Karp's life was fading away on the operating table and there was no time to present requests to the various groups. Dr. Cooley was also accused of being very secretive about the surgery. Even Dr. Michael E. DeBakey, head of the Baylor-Rice program, where the heart was developed, was unaware of Dr. Cooley's plans. Later, Dr. DeBakey criticized Dr. Cooley for going ahead too soon and without approval.

The next time ethical issues connected with implantation arose was in the Barney Clark case. Clark met the standards set up by the University of Utah's Institutional Review Board (IRB), the FDA, and the selection committee of the medical center. However, experts still disagree on whether or not Clark was the right candidate.

One point discussed is that Clark was a heavy smoker and had been sick with a lung condition for a long time. A patient in better health might have had a better chance of recovery. Would not such a recipient have taught the doctors more about the artificial heart?

Another argument is that Clark's social class, economic level, education, religion, and skin color were the same as the doctors. Did these factors influence the patient selection process?

Debate continues over who should sit on the review boards that monitor heart implantations. After Clark's death, the Utah IRB demanded that Dr. DeVries explain what went wrong. They delayed approval of his second operation for a year. Dr. DeVries grew impatient and moved to Humana-Audubon Hospital. It took the review board there only six weeks to give permission for a second implantation.

"I am suspicious of their [the Humana Hospital's review board] independence," said Arthur Kaplan of the Hastings Center, a leading think tank on matters of medical ethics. "They have had little experience in reviewing research and . . . most work directly at the hospital. That is different from Utah in that a fair proportion [of their IRB] was not affiliated with the hospital."

THERAPY OR RESEARCH?

Dr. DeVries has said that in Barney Clark's case he had the "dubious distinction" of trying to make up his mind on whether the chief purpose of the operation was primarily therapeutic or experimental. Later he said, "Our first concern was benefit [to the patient], not utilitarianism."

The surgeon has been criticized for not being straight in his own mind on the main purpose of the implantations. Was the main goal to benefit the subjects and the second goal to gain new knowledge—or the other way around?

Dr. George J. Annas, professor of health law at Boston University School of Medicine, said: "Some days he [Dr. DeVries] says he is doing it [operating] to benefit patients. Their choice is to have this or die. He doesn't talk about them being human guinea pigs, which is really what they are . . . their lives are clearly secondary. Medical research is clearly first."

One leading medical ethicist, Dr. Albert R. Jonsen of the University of California, San Francisco, claims that the goal of clinical research is mainly utilitarian. The aim is to gather information that will help future patients, not necessarily benefit the subjects themselves. To select only sub-

[82]

jects whose health will be improved by the experiment is not the way to advance science, he believes. In his view, "the next series of implants will still be experimental; we cannot expect much therapeutic benefit for the sufferers. At most, you have a hope of benefit."

Opinions on human experimentation go back a long way. In the third century, the Roman physician and philosopher, Cornelius Celsus, approved of the vivisection of criminals for research. He said, "It is not cruel to inflict on a few criminals sufferings which may benefit multitudes of innocent persons throughout the ages."

Claude Bernard, the nineteenth-century father of experimental medicine, stated the other side of the argument: "The principle of medical morality consists in never performing on man an experiment that might be harmful to him to any extent, though the results might be highly advantageous to science and to the health of others."

In regard to the question of whether or not a doctor is justified in taking all possible steps, no matter how hopeless the situation seems, to save the life of a dying patient, Dr. Francis D. Moore of the Harvard Medical School wrote in his 1972 book *Transplant*: "The answer to this question must be negative. . . . It raises false hopes . . . calls into discredit all of biomedical science, and it gives the impression that physicians and surgeons are adventurers rather than circumspect persons seeking to help the suffering and dying by the use of hopeful measures."

QUALITY OF LIFE

Eleven seriously ill heart patients were interviewed at the time of Barney Clark's surgery. Ten said that given the chance, they too would choose the artificial heart. The only one who disagreed was a twenty-nine-year-old man. He had undergone a human heart transplant the year before. If he had it to do over again, he said, he would refuse the transplant because his "quality of life" was so poor.

Quality of life is an extremely difficult term to define

in precise terms. Transplant and implant patients might say that a good quality of life means being able to live as they had lived before they got sick. Others might include in the definition the activities—from walking and running to playing at various sports to going on trips—that most people of the same age can do.

The Utah IRB debated the quality of life issue in Barney Clark's case. Successful implantations would mean that Clark would be tethered to the large, clumsy heart driver for the rest of his life. But he was a dying man. Would not any sort of life, no matter what quality, be better than death?

The IRB insisted that Clark be told how limited his future life would be. They also warned him to expect a life of "discomfort, need for follow-up tests, possible future operations, and so forth."

Members of the team that treated Clark had different definitions of a successful outcome. Some declared it would be a success if Clark survived the operation. Others said success would mean surviving for several years. Dr. DeVries said that for the procedure to be called a success, "the patient must say it was worth it."

When he was feeling well, Clark did, in fact, say that it was "worth it." At several other times, though, Clark was so depressed that he asked to be allowed to die. His wife regarded the experiment as only a "partial success."

To some, the artificial heart is a success because four of the five end-stage patients who received the device had their lives extended for months or years. But to those who focus on quality of life, it is probably a failure. All the recipients suffered strokes, were limited in their activities by the heart driver, and spent most of their life in a hospital—which is a very poor quality of life indeed.

One ethicist posed this question: "Did Barney Clark live for 112 days or was he dying for 112 days?" Some people accused the medical team of playing God for no better reason than to satisfy their own egos and ambitions and to further their research. But Dr. Willem Kolff, head of the University of Utah team, disagrees: "It's not our duty to determine if the life is worth living—just to do what we can."

Dr. Ross Woolley, a member of the Utah IRB, wrote in the *New England Journal of Medicine*: "Dr. Barney Clark clearly did not achieve the level of function he or the experimentors had hoped for. . . . There were certain inadequacies and errors in what we did, but they represented ignorance of the unknown rather than acts of arrogance or neglect."

The artificial heart is proving useful in a way the original designers had not imagined. Once looked on as a permanent replacement for a diseased heart, it is now being used more as a temporary bridge to keep patients alive until a human heart can be found. For that reason, the FDA, which is the government agency that regulates medical experimentation, is allowing implants of the artificial heart.

INFORMED CONSENT

Before starting any human experimental or therapeutic procedure, the doctor must first obtain the person's permission. This is usually done by asking the person, or a guardian if the patient is a child, to sign a consent form. These forms are standard for most procedures. But some of the usual clauses take on different meanings when dealing with artificial heart implants.

Most experts agree that to be really informed the patient must have the procedure fully explained, including any and all experimental elements. He or she must be told of the risks and benefits, any pain and discomfort to be expected, and all possible alternatives. All of the patient's questions have to be answered. And finally, it must be made clear that the patient can refuse at any point to go through with the implantation.

Informed consent agreements usually include a "freedom-to-withdraw" item. This gives the subject the right to

[85]

get out of the experiment or therapy whenever he or she wants. This, of course, presents certain difficulties in an artificial heart implant. To ask that the artificial heart be removed is to ask help in committing suicide.

"Implied promise of benefit" is also part of most informed consent forms. It tells the subject what the doctors expect to gain as a result of the procedure. When dealing with the artificial heart, however, it is important for the patient to realize that the doctors simply don't know what benefit the patient will get with the implant.

Particularly important for the artificial heart patient is the "financial considerations" portion. The actual implantation costs many thousands of dollars. And high medical bills continue as long as the device is in place. About one-half of all health insurance companies will pay for a heart transplant; but most will not cover the cost of an implant, since they consider that procedure experimental, not therapeutic.

The external support system of the artificial heart, at its present stage of development, needs constant attention. This is usually provided by the recipient's family. Therefore the "role of relatives" clause is particularly important for artificial heart implants.

The consent form given to Barney Clark was eleven pages long. After his death, many experts said they felt that the form was not adequate. Two points were lacking, they claimed. The form made no provision for decisions to be made in case Clark was either mentally incompetent or under anesthesia. Clark's wife made the decisions when he could not. But he should have had the chance to name the person. Also, he asked several times to be allowed to die. How should that have been handled? Did it fall under the freedom-to-withdraw clause? Should his wish have been honored?

Since Barney Clark, the informed consent forms for artificial heart implants have grown to be seventeen pages long. They cover some points that had been missing. The new forms emphasize the experimental nature of implantation, the uncertain outcome, and the many ways the device will restrict the patient's style of living.

The question of whether or not informed consent is realistic remains. Can a patient who is told that his or her only possible treatment would be an artificial heart do anything but agree? How can the patient be informed if even the doctors are not too sure what to expect?

In his autobiography, Philip Blaiberg, who was Dr. Christiaan Barnard's second heart transplant recipient, recalls that Dr. Barnard asked him to go through with the operation not only for his own sake but also for Barnard's.

Clark's case was similar. After reading through the informed consent form together with Dr. DeVries, Clark looked up with a grin and said, "All I can say is, there'd be a lot of long faces around here if I backed out now." Clark knew that he had really given his consent when he arrived at the hospital. The informing had taken place before he even entered the hospital.

COST OF HUMAN LIFE

Experts estimate that each artificial heart implantation costs at least $75,000, and that between 15,000 and 40,000 people each year are candidates for the procedure. The widespread use of artificial hearts, therefore, could cost an estimated $3 billion! Daniel J. Callahan, director of the Hastings Center, comments, "It's a very large amount of money for the quality of life you get."

The actual cost may be much higher. Dr. Kolff, for instance, thinks more in terms of up to 100,000 artificial heart implants a year. This means many billions of dollars for medical care at a time of widespread budget cuts and government economies. As Dr. Lewis Thomas, the well-known medical researcher and writer, asked, "And where is the money to come from, at a time when every penny

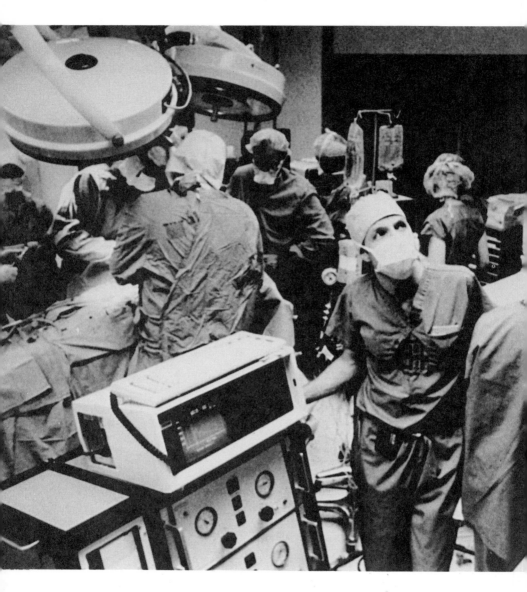

*Large teams of doctors, nurses, and technicians
are involved in heart transplant or implant operations,
making them very expensive procedures.*

of taxpayer's money for the health care system is being pinched out of shape?"

The government is now involved in deciding to what extent health insurance and social welfare systems should provide funds for implants or transplants. In June 1986, the federal Medicare system agreed to cover a limited number of heart transplants. It is estimated that there will be 143 transplants a year under Medicare at a cost of $25 million.

Many points still remain to be decided. Does the government guarantee of a minimum level of health care include heart implants and transplants? Should some of these operations be excluded? Which ones? How is it decided if a transplant or implant is experimental or therapeutic?

Since the cost of each implantation is so very high, some people are asking whether the money would not be better spent on efforts to prevent heart disease, instead of providing hearts for just a few people. Dr. Hatcher speaks for many doctors when he says, "I would rather see the money going for learning about how to prevent the conditions that lead to end-stage heart disease. I hope we could solve those problems before we contemplate having tens of thousands of people walking around with these complex units that require whole teams to service.

Many people who abuse their health by smoking, drinking heavily, or eating poorly need mechanical hearts. Should the government use tax money to pay for their devices? Yet if the government does not pay, will only the very rich be able to afford them?

Questions about the ethics of artificial heart implants have a way of raising more questions. It is obvious that there are no quick, easy answers to any of them. But it is vital to establish a set of guiding principles. Doctors and medical ethicists, patients and their families, government agencies and insurance companies, and the public at large are all striving to arrive at a fair, moral policy on these issues.

9

PSYCHOLOGICAL

ISSUES

Suppose you are fifty or sixty years old. You are suffering from serious heart disease. Despite years of treatment your condition is steadily growing worse. Your doctor tells you that your only hope is an artificial heart implant. It will keep you alive until a donor heart comes along. What would you do?

If you are like most people, you would probably agree to the bridge-to-transplant operation. What you might not realize is that many people with heart implants or transplants develop psychological problems. Although these problems are usually not physically disabling, the mental and emotional distress can have a powerful impact on the recipients and the people around them.

Transplant or implant surgery can uproot families, wreck financial, career, and education plans, and strain personal relationships. The long periods of fear and uncertainty also lead to higher rates of suicide and divorce among transplantees.

Because there are so many more heart transplants than implants, most of the psychological studies have been done on transplantees. The issues and concerns, though, are believed to be similar.

THE SCREENING
OF PATIENTS

One important issue the experts are trying to resolve is: What kind of people make the best adjustment to heart implants or transplants? The shortage of donor hearts, for example, has created a strong need to choose candidates who will gain most from a new organ. The knowledge researchers are gaining from these psychological studies will help in setting up guidelines to aid in the patient selection process.

Most candidates for heart implantation or transplantation are interviewed by psychologists or psychiatrists. The purpose is to screen out people with serious mental conditions, such as depression or psychosis. Dr. Norman B. Levy of the New York Medical College believes that such people tend to be poor risks for these operations.

The interviews also evaluate the patient's psychological and emotional stability. The well-adjusted candidate is thought best able to go through the surgery and cooperate in the postoperative treatment. Further, this person may also contribute more effectively to the study of his or her condition.

Dr. John Mount, chief of psychiatry at St. Joseph's Hospital in London, Canada, holds a different viewpoint. Dr. Mount believes that emotionally troubled patients should not be automatically excluded from consideration. Many psychological problems can be overcome, he says. And he is optimistic about most patients' chances of success, even if they are suffering from some psychological disturbance.

Says Dr. Jack G. Copeland of the University of Arizona, "My own feeling is that almost anybody is a reasonable candidate for transplantation. There are very few adults who are not capable of coping with the stresses. We don't need an all-American boy with a supportive wife and family, well-to-do, from a white, upper-class situation to get a success. Almost anyone who has faced the alternative of death or transplantation can do it."

ADJUSTMENT PROBLEMS
FOR PATIENTS

A human heart transplant does not end when the patient is wheeled out of the operating room. The condition lasts forever. The operation may affect every aspect of the recipient's life—from appearance to personality.

Patients are required to continue taking drugs for life to prevent organ rejection and other complications. They must also adjust to a completely new body image. "That most maintain their sanity is a tribute to human fortitude," says Dr. Paul Keoun of University Hospital in London, Canada.

A 1984 study of forty heart transplant patients described one young man who had a transplant but did not make a very good adjustment. Like many other transplant patients, he failed to foresee how it would interfere with his return to a normal life. "If I had known then what I know now," he said, "I probably would have declined the surgery." Despite informed consent and detailed explanations of what he would face, he was unprepared for the bad feelings that have stayed with him.

Marjorie Rorabough, a 1979 heart transplantee, was quoted as saying that she "hates" the way she looks. The medication she must take leaves her face puffy and moon-shaped. "I'm a completely different person, and I didn't really expect that. My eyes bulge, I look pregnant all the time, I bruise if you touch me and have onion skin like a ninety-year-old. I'd give anything, almost, to get rid of this. I don't even look at myself in the mirror. I guess you don't get someone else's heart without paying for it."

Yet, despite the high psychological price of transplants, most recipients still come out strongly on the side of the transplant. Rorabough, when asked to describe her current emotional state, said: "On a scale of one to ten, with ten tops, I'd rate mine at nine and a half!"

Patients have trouble adjusting to the "alien" organ inside their body. They face a double challenge: coping with the loss of a body part and accepting a new one.

A Maine woman was very upset by the prospect of having her heart removed and replaced by that of a stranger's. She had to be talked into it. Later she said to her sister, "I will always have a person walking beside me."

Recipients pass through various stages as they adjust to the transplant. Failure to do so may lead to psychological, as well as physical, rejection of the new heart.

The first stage is one of great relief and happiness. Patients have a sense of rebirth and renewal, "like a new-born child," says one Johns Hopkins Hospital social worker. "They think everything they see and touch is sensational."

But then other feelings arise. During the second stage they suffer nagging doubts and worries. The recipients are very frightened and become overly conscious of every heartbeat and flutter. One patient even began carrying around a stethoscope until his wife took it away!

The third stage is characterized by depression, denial, and guilt. A California nurse, for instance, has the heart of a nineteen-year-old boy. Every year, on the anniversary of his death, she sends an azalea plant to his mother. But to this day her gifts have never been acknowledged. "I would like one day to be able to talk to them [his parents] to tell them what this has meant to me," she says. "It still troubles me very much."

At this time, also, many patients begin to experience the realities that they didn't want to hear about before surgery. They try to repress disturbing thoughts about the "alien" heart in their body. But then they suffer guilt over the denial.

[93]

Experts say the feelings of being disappointed and psychologically uncomfortable are common. But these feelings need not be permanent. In the more successful cases, the patient goes on to the fourth and final stage. This is described as a time of being at peace with the new heart. It results in a good adjustment to the differences between the hopes and the realities of the transplantation.

The process of integrating the heart transplant or implant into the psyche has been described by Dr. Hyman Muslin of the University of Illinois Medical School as "special changes in the perception of their self" that the patients undergo. "The psychological changes of a person with a new organ are akin to the changes of someone who goes through a stage of life such as adolescence, when their own organs . . . are experienced as being not in concert with other parts of their body."

After a heart transplant one young patient refused to remove his baseball cap. Without his cap, he told the therapist, "people wouldn't be able to recognize me, because I lost my heart. They only know me by my heart."

Some patients who receive the heart of another person react as though they have received what Dr. Muslin calls a "psychological implant." The person takes on some of the personality and character—real or imagined—of the donor. The recipient behaves as if the donor now exists within his or her body. If the donor was artistic, the recipient may show a greater interest in painting. If the donor was generous, the recipient may share things more willingly than before.

This change of personality, when it works well, may lead to a better sense of self. "Often," says Dr. Muslin, "they [the recipients] go from a state of low vigor and self-esteem to a much better psychological state. . . ." But this change also has certain risks. It may result in depression or some other form of mental illness. Dr. Pietro Castelnuovo-Tedesco, a Vanderbilt University psychiatrist, observes that "a new organ . . . leads to thoughts of having robbed the donor of a vital part, thoughts accompanied by guilt and fears of punishment and retaliation."

ADJUSTMENT PROBLEMS FOR RELATIVES

The family of the recipient is also deeply affected by the implant or transplant surgery. And their relationships with the patient have always been considered very important for good adjustment.

One of the reasons that the patient selection committee chose Barney Clark was because they believed that his family's love and support would help him through the ordeal. One forty-eight-year-old man, who was an excellent candidate in all other respects, was turned down because the committee thought that no one in his family cared much "whether he lived or died."

Lack of family support is one of the most frequent reasons for disqualifying patients. Yet no one has ever questioned or tested this requirement. It may be unfair to refuse new hearts to patients just because they do not have a family or have poor family relationships.

Dr. David Reiss, a psychiatrist at George Washington University, challenges the notion that family support is a vital factor. He considers it possible that someone without a family might make an even better patient, since he or she would be free of family pressures and problems.

This new way of thinking is leading to some changes in the patient selection process. Homosexuals, for example, are no longer automatically rejected. Divorcees, also, are now eligible to receive transplants.

Barney Clark's wife, Una Loy, shared her husband's "strong desire to serve and fulfill his mission." And she helped to sustain Clark and the heart team by means of her unwavering support. Yet even she has talked of the stress on her and the rest of her family during her husband's sickness, surgery, and life with a heart implant. Despite

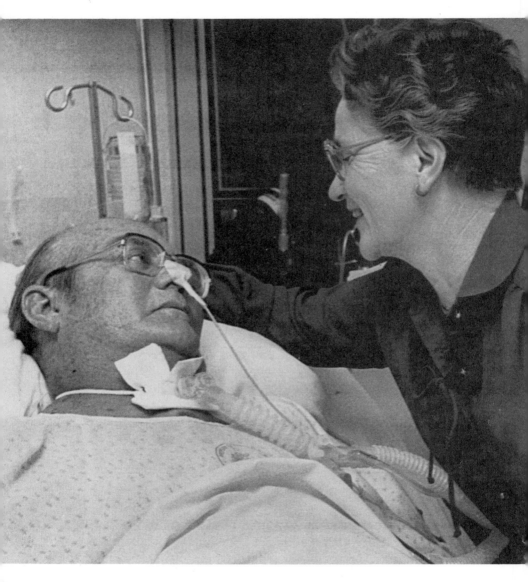

*Barney Clark's devoted wife, Una Loy,
was part of the reason Clark was chosen
to become an artificial heart recipient.*

her courage and dedication, the constant threat of death created anxiety. According to Dr. Reiss, this tension is felt very strongly in close-knit families. It may be harder for devoted families to deal with separation and loss than for open families, whose members are less involved with one another.

Oddly enough, illness holds some families together. There have been instances where the family actually fell apart when the patient returned to good health. "A lot of transplantees have real problems with their wives and others who never want them to take risks or do anything physical," says Floyd Winget, a heart transplantee from Fort Wayne, Indiana. To help transplantees combat this problem Winget has organized a self-help group of heart recipients.

Strong reactions to the new heart recipient sometimes extend to the workplace. "Employers are terrified," one hospital public relations staffer commented, "that a heart transplant will suddenly be rejected in the middle of the factory floor and explode out of the chest. They can't deal with it."

ADJUSTMENT PROBLEMS
FOR THE MEDICAL TEAM

The doctors, nurses, researchers, and technicians also become emotionally involved with transplant and implant patients. In the words of Dr. Chase Peterson, a spokesperson for the University of Utah Medical Center at the time of Barney Clark's implantation, "We are overwhelmed with responsibility for Dr. Clark."

After Clark's death, members of the team that developed the device, did the surgery, and cared for him afterward, questioned whether they had done the right thing. Renee C. Fox and Judith P. Swazey spoke to the team as part of a sociological study of the Clark heart implant. They found that the staff had an "it-was-the-best-of-times-

and-the-worst-of-times" feeling about it. Some were also concerned about the impression given that Clark received more attention than other patients.

A social worker at the Johns Hopkins Hospital describes some of the joy of being part of a transplant experience. She tells what it was like to sit with the family of a heart-transplant candidate awaiting the arrival of the donor heart by helicopter: "The room was dim, the patient's mother was saying her rosary. Except for the click of the beads, it was quiet. We heard the chopper, then saw the ship hover over the brightly lit harbor, blinking its lights as it landed on the heliport roof of the hospital. We knew that young man's heart was coming, his new life. No one could say a word. It was one of the emotional highs of my life."

While there are many highs, the medical staff must also deal with frequent lows. Patients often suffer setbacks and pass through numerous life-and-death crises. These times can be psychologically very difficult for the professional staff.

Surgeons are rarely prepared to handle the emotional state of their patients. They are often unable to cope with their own emotional turmoil, let alone counsel transplant patients. Most surgeons are used to dealing with patients over a short stretch of time only. Some feel uncomfortable with the long-term contact that transplants and implants bring.

Additional pressure comes from the fact that implants and transplants are so newsworthy. "The stresses play an important role in the outcomes of transplant programs," says Dr. Copeland. "There's the publicity, the need to maintain a program always up to snuff, and constant fear of uncertainty."

Many medical staff members have their own psychological problems. Yet patients depend on them for emotional support and guidance. The hospital staff has to deal with three basic types of personalities. There are the "dependent" patients. They lean heavily on the staff to satisfy all their physical and psychological needs. Virtually helpless, these patients place great demands on the people around them.

The "independent" patients try to take charge of their own cases. Hospital workers often find them very hard to handle. One common trait of this group is to question almost everything the doctors or nurses do. Independent patients, however, usually make a good psychological adjustment when they are discharged.

The third group, the "adaptive" patients, are perhaps the smallest in number. While in the hospital they tend to be cooperative and undemanding. But when they return home, they become fully independent and self-directed.

Some situations put a particular psychological strain on the transplant or implant team. The death of a heart recipient or the decision to refuse to treat a patient who is close to death poses special emotional problems for the medical staff.

There is also the difficult task given to doctors and nurses on the "organ-harvesting squads." They are the ones who ask families for organ donations. How difficult it must be to ask grieving relatives to donate the organs of a loved one who has just died! The best donors are young, otherwise healthy men and women who are killed accidentally, frequently in a car or motorcycle wreck. This makes it all the more painful for the victims' families, and all the more trying for the ones requesting the donation. Yet they must ask because those who are accidentally killed are the most valuable source for transplant organs. Says one organ-harvesting squad member, "We wait like vultures."

Almost every transplant and implant team includes a psychologist or psychiatrist to help in the selection of candidates and to counsel the patients and their families. But many experts are calling for much greater involvement of the mental health professionals. They would like to see more psychological research done on patients, their families, and the medical teams. And they would like psychologists or psychiatrists to be on hand to help the medical people handle the intense stress.

Psychologist Leonard Perlman sums up the need to offer more psychological help to everyone connected with transplantation: "The priorities of the psychological and psychiatric professions must change to put organ transplantation up higher. The population is staying alive to older ages, and transplantation will be in even greater demand. We now hold out the promise of a normative life for these people. But until we recognize their need for psychological services, we can't be sure their lives will be richer as well as longer."

LESSONS LEARNED

In October 1983, a three-day conference to evaluate the University of Utah's artificial heart program was held in Houston, Texas. Some interesting points about the psychology of recipients came out of this conference.

To be accepted, candidates must demonstrate a history of medical compliance. That is, they have to show a cooperative attitude toward doctors and a willingness to accept what the doctors say or do without question. There is now some doubt about whether this is desirable. Studies show that patients who get angry, complain, question, and challenge the course of their treatment often recover faster and make a better psychological adjustment in the long run.

Barney Clark was chosen for the first heart implant because he was considered psychologically and emotionally strong. As we said, Clark may also have been selected because his social, economic, religious, and family background were most like that of the surgeons and physicians. Dr. Keoun said that sometimes psychological factors tend to be linked with social factors. "I have a deep suspicion," he says, "that we make subjective assessments based on some outmoded ideas about families and support. What would *your* selection be if the choice was between a university-educated father of three with high social status and a twenty-five-year-old with a history of drug abuse, disorderly conduct, and limited intelligence?"

In their book, *The Courage to Fail,* Fox and Swazey wrote that the physician-patient relationship is an important part of organ transplantation programs. "Confronting this situation [possible death for the patient] with courage is an ultimate value shared by physicians and patients." A "we-shall-overcome" attitude challenges everyone to persevere and triumph over great odds.

As we said at the beginning of this book, some people compare Barney Clark to "Columbus on a voyage of discovery." Others, like Dr. Albert R. Jonsen of the University of California, San Francisco, consider Dr. DeVries the real explorer. No doubt both will long be remembered for their exceptional achievements. Clark's sense of being on a medical "adventure" gave him the courage to continue. And Dr. DeVries' medical skill, optimism, and inner strength held everyone together. The key to the success of future implants may have more to do with such hard-to-test special qualities as these in patients and their doctors than with anything else.

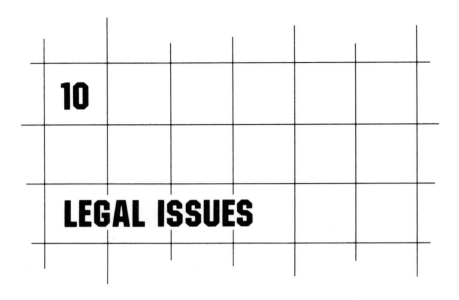

10

LEGAL ISSUES

A sixty-two-year-old man collapses on the street. Someone calls an ambulance, which takes him to a hospital. The only way the doctors can save his life is by immediate surgery. They rush him to the operating room.

All this time the man remains unconscious. He cannot be asked to sign a consent form. During the surgery his heart fails. The surgeons know he will die unless they give him a new heart. He is too old to receive a transplant. So they implant an artificial heart.

Hours later the man wakes up. He discovers that he has had a heart implant. The patient says that he does not want to be tethered to an outside source of power for life.

What can he do? Does he have the right to turn off the device and die? Is the doctor at fault for doing the implantation without a signed consent form and prior government approval? What are the legal issues that apply to artificial heart implantation?

DECISIONS AND DYING

As yet there has not been an artificial heart implantation in an unwilling recipient. But it almost came up in the case of Mary Lund. In December 1985, Lund became the first woman to get an artificial heart. Dying from congestive heart failure, she was too weak to sign the informed consent form. Her husband signed for her.

After the surgery Lund lapsed into a coma. A week later she awoke and was shocked to learn that she had received an artificial heart. In this particular case, the issue of turning off the device was avoided because the patient received a donor heart forty-five days later.

Some hospitals have a policy on ending, or the termination of, treatment. Dr. William DeVries, speaking for the Humana Heart Institute International, says, "If a guy wakes up with an artificial heart and becomes a permanent patient and doesn't want it, he should be able to turn off the device."

At Abbott Northwestern Hospital in Minneapolis, where Lund was a patient, doctors claim they would try to persuade a patient not to withdraw from treatment. But if this were to fail, they would be prepared to honor the patient's wishes and turn off the artificial heart.

The Hershey Medical Center, the Texas Heart Institute, the Presbyterian University Hospital in Pittsburgh, and the University of Arizona Medical Center in Tucson are four major medical centers doing transplant surgery. None of them has publicly announced a policy on termination of treatment.

The issue of who is to make decisions when the patient is unable was not covered in the consent form that Barney Clark signed. Utah, though, is one of forty-two states that has a law covering this situation. It states that when a patient is incompetent, the closest relative has the power to act in his or her behalf. Of course, this includes the decision to end treatment.

Alexander Morgan Capron, professor of law and ethics at Georgetown University, considers the language of the informed consent agreement too vague on this point. For example, one statement reads: "I understand I am free at any time to withdraw my consent to participate in this experimental project, recognizing that the exercise of such an option after the artificial heart is in place may result in my death." Capron calls this "unclear and evasive." Does it specifically mean that the patient can have the artificial heart turned off even if the doctors advise otherwise?

Dr. DeVries has said that he personally would have no problem with honoring the request of a patient to shut off the device. The only difficulty would be in making sure the patient truly wanted it stopped. On the few occasions that Barney Clark said that he wanted to die, Dr. DeVries decided that they were not serious requests. He considered them just a reaction to the pain or depression Clark was feeling at the time. Dr. DeVries has also said that most doctors have their own standards about when to follow such wishes and when to ignore them.

Another important legal issue came out of the Barney Clark case. It concerns the responsibility of the university or hospital if a patient decides to withdraw from treatment. With artificial hearts, shutting off the machine is really committing suicide. Since it is so difficult to know a patient's true intentions, the institution would probably be at some risk, legally speaking, says Capron.

Researchers who do experimental procedures focus all of their attention on making them succeed. They seldom think about the patient dying, and even less about what is called the "quality of death." As Dr. Albert R. Jonsen, prominent medical ethicist, said: "Because the heart team wanted Clark to live so badly, they may not have confronted the quality of his death completely."

Experts are calling for guidelines to help doctors decide when a patient's desire to die should be taken seriously. Once the rules are set, researchers will not have to worry so much over legal suits accusing them of murder or of contributing to a suicide.

The debate on when to end life is complicated. How should patients be protected both from those who might wish them dead and from those who might want to prolong

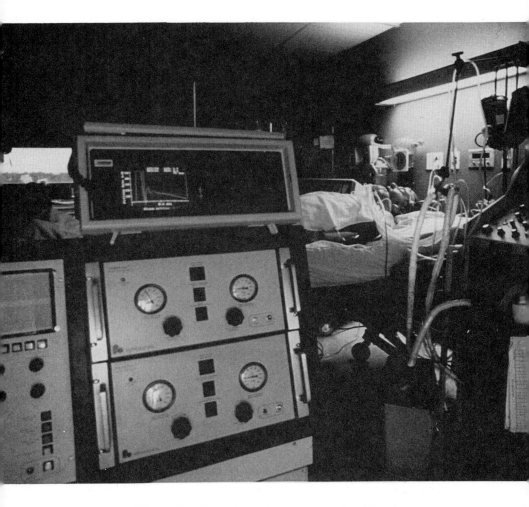

There is a lot of equipment involved in
maintaining an artificial heart. On the
left side of the picture is the heart driver,
a machine critical to the system and to
which the patient must remain permanently
tethered. This makes many people question
the quality of life possible under
current artificial heart technology.

their lives for selfish motives? How can society define something as personal as quality of death? Should it? As attorney and physician Dr. Richard S. Scott has said: "One man's heaven-sent three extra weeks of life in bed connected to tubes and machines is another man's living hell."

A right-to-die group in New York City, Concern for Dying, says there is a "coercion of fear" in most hospitals. Doctors, hospital lawyers, and administrators often suggest to families and patients that it is somehow criminal to exercise their constitutional rights. The group is filing lawsuits on behalf of patients. They are seeking monetary damages from doctors and hospitals for not honoring the patients' refusal of further treatment. At the same time they are calling for new laws that will "fill in the holes created ... by a technology that is advancing faster than any court or legislature."

GOVERNMENT-APPROVED IMPLANTS

The Food and Drug Administration (FDA) is the federal government agency that licenses new medical devices, such as the artificial heart. It requires a full description of the device and procedures before approving the use of an experimental device on a human being.

As of this writing, Dr. DeVries has done four (Barney Clark, William Schroeder, Murray Haydon, and Jack Burcham) of the seven permanent implants for which he has received FDA permission. There is no time limit on completion of the series. In January 1986, the agency said it would review the results of each case before allowing Dr. DeVries to proceed. This means that the implantations could be stopped at any time if they feel that the artificial heart is not safe or is not advancing research.

Some consider the FDA rules a sound way of regulating experimentation with the artificial heart. They say it gives the researchers the most knowledge at the smallest possible risk and pain to the patients.

But others disagree. Dr. DeVries believes there is too much regulation. He fears it may stifle the experimentation that is necessary to advance the science of medicine. In one interview he pointed out that the United States is falling behind other nations in the amount of published research on artificial organs. The developer of the most popular artificial heart model, Dr. Robert K. Jarvik, also complains that surgeons have to "sit on their hands while the FDA shuffles paper."

One particular area of concern for the FDA is the use of artificial hearts as a bridge to transplant. They have given four hospitals permission to do a total of thirty-seven bridge transplants. Senator Albert Gore of Tennessee and other members of Congress recently called on the FDA to limit the number of bridge-to-transplant procedures. "The bridge takes donor hearts away from a proven heart-transplant program," said Senator Gore. "We must assume that a good potential recipient elsewhere will die every single time a donor heart goes to a bridge patient." The FDA has not yet responded to this charge.

Critics of the bridge program worry that too many procedures are based on "halfway technology." They also suggest that those on artificial hearts may not be the best transplant candidates. Often these patients are at the highest risk with the least chance of long-term survival.

Dr. Abhijit Acharya, of the FDA's Division of Cardiovascular Services, however, insists that the bridge program is being well handled. Dr. John Pennock of the Hershey Medical Center also strongly approves of the FDA bridge program. In March 1986, he said: "What we need to do is carry out the experiment and follow patients for at least two years. Then we will know if their survival rate equals that of patients who have gotten the transplant alone." So far all the figures seem to bear him out.

Senator Gore also had his doubts on the selection of the hospitals to do the bridges. Some have only just begun implantations and lack proven programs. In a few cases hospitals have used artificial hearts without approval.

Dr. Acharya is trying to deal with the situation. "But when a doctor calls and says the patient is dying on the table, we can't say yes or no. We tell him, 'You do what is best in your medical judgment. But be aware of the laws. The FDA may take action after the fact.' "

IMPLANTS WITHOUT GOVERNMENT APPROVAL

The case of Thomas Creighton illustrates a situation where an artificial heart was implanted without FDA permission. Creighton was an auto mechanic from Tucson, Arizona. He suffered his first heart attack at age thirty. In March 1985, at age thirty-three, he entered the University of Arizona Medical Center to await a heart transplant.

On March 5, Dr. Jack G. Copeland gave Creighton a donor heart. But the transplant failed. Creighton nearly died of cardiac arrest. For seven-and-a-half hours he was kept alive on a heart-lung machine while doctors searched for another heart donor. None could be found.

Not seeing any other solution, Dr. Copeland called Dr. Willem Kolff in Utah for a Jarvik-7 device. Dr. Kolff agreed to send one on the very next plane. But Creighton's condition continued to worsen. The Jarvik-7 would arrive too late. So the troubled Dr. Copeland asked Kevin Cheng, a dentist, for the artificial heart that he had developed. This so-called Phoenix heart was designed to be implanted in a calf, had never been tested in a human, and lacked FDA approval.

Dr. Copeland called the FDA for permission to implant the Phoenix heart. Although he was turned down, he went ahead with the operation.

THE PHOENIX HEART

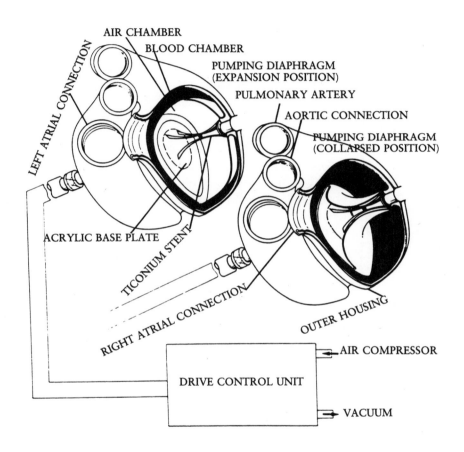

AIR CHAMBER
BLOOD CHAMBER
PUMPING DIAPHRAGM
(EXPANSION POSITION)
PULMONARY ARTERY
AORTIC CONNECTION
PUMPING DIAPHRAGM
(COLLAPSED POSITION)
LEFT ATRIAL CONNECTION
ACRYLIC BASE PLATE
TICONIUM STENT
RIGHT ATRIAL CONNECTION
OUTER HOUSING
AIR COMPRESSOR
DRIVE CONTROL UNIT
VACUUM

The Phoenix artificial heart

The next day a donor heart was found. Dr. Copeland removed the artificial heart and put the human heart in its place. But this second human heart also developed complications. Creighton died of heart failure on the following day.

Some consider Dr. Copeland a medical hero. He did everything humanly possible to save Creighton's life—even if it meant breaking the law. That Creighton only lived an extra day or two didn't matter. But to others, such as Dr. George J. Annas, an authority on health law, "what happened at Tucson was bizarre. It shouldn't have happened. But it probably will happen again."

According to FDA rules, any institution that ignores its regulations can be barred from taking part in FDA-supervised research. The agency could punish him, and the University of Arizona, even though he implanted the heart in an effort to save a man's life.

The FDA struck a compromise by "applying a very strict law in a compassionate way." William Grigg, spokesperson for the FDA, said that the agency would not impose penalties on Dr. Copeland or the University of Arizona. In return, university officials promised to get approval before the next implantation.

The Creighton incident recalls the dispute that arose after the first artificial heart implantation in Haskell Karp. Dr. Michael E. DeBakey had led the team that developed an artificial heart under the Baylor-Rice Artificial Heart Program. But Dr. Denton Cooley, without informing anyone, took the artificial heart from the lab and used it for the Karp implantation.

Dr. DeBakey later said that the heart was "not ready for implantation." He further explained: "The artificial heart was covertly taken from the Baylor Labs to St. Luke's Hospital in Houston where it was used in human experiment on April 4, 1969, without prior approval of the institutional human research committee or by the responsible investigator of the project under which the device was developed."

Dr. Cooley's defense was simple. His patient was dying. The artificial heart might save his life. There was no time to bother with red tape. "If a man is overboard and someone throws him a life preserver," Cooley later said, "he's not going to inspect it and see if it has a guarantee."

Haskell Karp's widow filed a medical malpractice suit against Dr. Cooley. The suit asked $4.5 million in damages. It was probably the first lawsuit dealing with an artificial heart. Mrs. Karp accused Dr. Cooley of making her husband "the unfortunate victim of human experimentation." Although Karp had signed an informed consent form, his widow said her husband was not truly informed. Dr. Cooley and the other doctors had "induced" Karp to undergo the implantation, she said.

The trial, *Karp v. Cooley*, began on June 19, 1972. It lasted ten days. Two of the judge's rulings made it difficult for Mrs. Karp to plead her case. One was that Dr. DeBakey could refuse to testify. The other was that Mrs. Karp's attorneys could not examine the Baylor-Rice laboratory records.

In the end, the court found Dr. Cooley innocent of medical negligence and declared that the operation was indeed therapy, not an experiment. Mrs. Karp lost again on appeal. Some experts wonder if the outcome will make it difficult for future implant recipients to obtain protection under the law.

In July 1981, Dr. Cooley became involved in a second, similar legal situation. That month Willebrordus Meuffels was flown from Holland to the Texas Heart Institute in Houston for a triple coronary bypass. Meuffels' heart started to fail during the operation.

Dr. Cooley asked Meuffels' wife to sign a consent form and implanted a new, experimental artificial heart in the patient. "There wasn't time to talk to committees and the

FDA, and I'm sorry," the surgeon said later. "I wasn't going to talk to his widow." Meuffels survived fifty-four hours on the artificial heart before getting a heart transplant. He lived just over a week with the human heart.

RIGHT TO PRIVACY

Dramatic new medical technologies like the artificial heart bring problems along with their many benefits. A chief difficulty has to do with informing the public and gaining public acceptance. Some efforts to win support for the artificial heart have turned into media events. The patients, their families, and the doctors and inventors have become celebrities. Reporters press for interviews and pictures.

How should the media balance the public's right to know with the patient's right to privacy? Most informed consent forms mention that the patient is expected to share information about the implant with the public. Should shy patients be denied implants if they are unwilling to speak to reporters? Or should patients be given a choice?

The public scrutiny surrounding artificial heart implants is quite new to most physicians, who are accustomed to guarding the confidentiality of their patients and to announcing their research findings in professional journals. The awkwardness and personal discomfort caused by all the exposure also makes any decision to terminate human experimentation much more difficult.

The conflict between the public's right to know and patients' privacy also shows up in the stories reporters write about heart implants. In their search for drama and excitement, the reporters may issue distorted accounts of the recipients' condition—making them appear either far healthier or sicker than they really are. They also may raise false hopes by exaggerating claims for the artificial heart.

The truth is that the artificial heart is not a miracle cure. It is the responsibility of journalists to present an

Sacramento Bee

'MR. SCHROEDER APPEARS TO BE SHOWING SIGNS OF WEARINESS. NEWS AT 11.'

accurate, balanced view, both of the patients' condition and the device.

Thus far, the doctors, patients, and courts have confronted only a very few of the many legal issues involved in artificial heart implants. The line separating the long-term needs of society and the personal interests of those involved in the implantation is still to be drawn.

[113]

ARTIFICIAL HEART IMPLANTS
(as of March 1987)

NAME	AGE	HOME	DATE OF IMPLANT	CHIEF SURGEON	
Haskell Karp	47	Skokie, IL	Apr. 4, 1969	Denton A. Cooley	
Willebrordus Meuffels	36	Holland	July 23, 1981	Denton A. Cooley	
Barney Clark	61	Seattle, WA	Dec. 2, 1982	William C. DeVries	
William Schroeder	53	Jasper, IN	Nov. 25, 1984	William C. DeVries	
Murray Haydon	58	Louisville, KY	Feb. 17, 1985	William C. DeVries	
Thomas Creighton	33	Tucson, AZ	Mar. 6, 1985	Jack G. Copeland	
Leif Stenberg	52	Sweden	Apr. 7, 1985	Bjarne Semb	
Jack Burcham	62	LeRoy, IL	Apr. 14, 1985	William C. DeVries	
Michael Drummond	25	Phoenix, AZ	Aug. 29, 1985	Jack G. Copeland	

HOSPITAL	DEVICE	COMMENTS
St. Luke's, Houston, TX	Baylor-Rice heart (Domingo Liotta)	Temporary. 64 hours on AH*; transplant Apr. 7, 1969; died Apr. 8, 1969, of pneumonia and kidney failure.
St. Luke's, Houston, TX	Baylor-Rice heart (Tetsuzo Akutsu)	Temporary. 54 hours on AH; transplant July 25, 1981; died Aug. 2, 1981, of infection and kidney and lung problems.
U. of Utah Med. Center, Salt Lake City, UT	Jarvik-7	Permanent. First permanent implantation. Lived for 112 days; died Mar. 23, 1983, of the failure of several organs.
Humana-Audubon, Louisville, KY	Jarvik-7	Permanent. Lived for 620 days, the longest survival of any permanent AH recipient to date. Died Aug. 6, 1986, of a series of strokes and lung infections.
Humana-Audubon, Louisville, KY	Jarvik-7	Permanent. Lived for 488 days; died June 19, 1986, of kidney failure.
U. of Ariz. Med. Center, Tucson, AZ	Phoenix heart (Kevin Cheng)	Temporary. Received heart transplant Mar. 5, 1985; transplant failed; given AH Mar. 6, 1985; 11 hours on AH; transplant that same day; died Mar. 8, 1985, of the failure of several organs.
Karolinska Inst., Stockholm, Sweden	Jarvik-7	Permanent. Lived 229 days; died Nov. 21, 1985, of a massive stroke.
Humana-Audubon, Louisville, KY	Jarvik-7	Permanent. Lived 10 days; died Apr. 24, 1985, of internal bleeding.
U. of Ariz. Med. Center, Tucson, AZ	Jarvik-7	Temporary. Youngest implant patient. 9 days on AH; transplant Sept. 7, 1985; left hospital Nov. 14, 1985. Living.

*Artificial Heart

NAME	AGE	HOME	DATE OF IMPLANT	CHIEF SURGEON	
Anthony Mandia	44	Philadelphia, PA	Oct. 18, 1985	William S. Pierce	
Thomas Gaidosh	47	Pittsburgh, PA	Oct. 24, 1985	Bartley P. Griffith	
Mary Lund	40	Kensington, MN	Dec. 19, 1985	Lyle Joyce	
Joseph Burello	39	Pittsburgh, PA	Feb. 3, 1986	Bartley P. Griffith	
Harris Kent	41	unknown	Feb. 3, 1986	unknown	
Bernadette Chayrez	40	Phoenix, AZ	Feb. 3, 1986	Jack G. Copeland	
Robert F. Cresswell	49	Huntingdon, PA	Mar. 17, 1986	William S. Pierce	
Gary Blake	43	East Liverpool, OH	Mar. 22, 1986	Bartley P. Griffith	
Edmund McDermott	32	unknown	June 13, 1986	Bartley P. Griffith	
Nicole Christoffersen	28	Minot, ND	Nov. 11, 1986	Lyle Joyce	
Ronald L. Smith	38	Gary, IN	Nov. 21, 1986	Alfred Tector	
Betty Shields	40	Sierra Vista, AZ	Nov. 26, 1986	Jack G. Copeland	

HOSPITAL	DEVICE	COMMENTS
Hershey Med. Center, Hershey, PA	Penn State heart	Temporary. 11 days on AH; transplant Oct. 28, 1985; died Nov. 14, 1985, of infection and the failure of several organs.
Presbyterian-U., Pittsburgh, PA	Jarvik-7	Temporary. 5 days on AH; transplant Oct. 28, 1985; left hospital Nov. 15, 1985. Living.
Abbott Northwestern Hospital, Minn., MN	Jarvik-7 (smaller version)	Temporary. First woman implant patient. Lived 43 days on AH; transplant Jan. 31, 1986. Died Oct. 14, 1986, of kidney failure.
Presbyterian-U., Pittsburgh, PA	Jarvik-7	Temporary. 13 days on AH; transplant Feb. 15, 1986. Living.
St. Luke's, Houston, TX	unknown	Not much known
U. of Ariz. Med. Center, Tucson, AZ	Jarvik-7 (smaller version)	Temporary. 4 days on AH; transplant Feb. 7, 1986; transplant failed; second AH implant Feb. 9, 1986. After 250 days Mrs. Chayrez, whose condition was worsening, asked for a human heart transplant. Died Oct. 11, 1986, during donor heart transplantation.
Hershey Med. Center, Hershey, PA	Penn State heart	Temporary. Received heart transplant Mar. 10, 1986; transplant failed.
Presbyterian-U., Pittsburgh, PA	Jarvik-7	Temporary. 17 days on AH; died Apr. 9, 1986, of lung infection while still awaiting a transplant.
Presbyterian-U., Pittsburgh, PA	Jarvik-7	Temporary. 8 days on AH; transplant June 21, 1986. Living.
Abbott Northwestern Hospital, Minn., MN	Jarvik-7 (smaller version)	Temporary. Awaiting a donor.
St. Luke's Hospital, Milw., WI	Jarvik-7	Temporary. 6 days on AH; transplant Nov. 26, 1986. Living.
U. of Ariz. Med. Center, Tucson, AZ	Jarvik-7 (smaller version)	Temporary. 8 days on AH; died Dec. 4, 1986, of multiple-organ failure.

GLOSSARY

Angina pectoris. Severe chest pain caused by a lack of blood supply to the heart muscles. The usual cause is a narrowing of the coronary arteries due to a buildup of fatty deposits. Also called angina.

Aorta. The main artery of the body. Blood is pumped into the aorta from the left ventricle of the heart, which carries it to all parts of the body except the lungs.

Aortic valve. See Semilunar valve.

Arterioles. Smaller arteries that branch off from the main arteries.

Arteriosclerosis. Hardening of the arteries. Any condition that causes the artery walls to thicken and lose elasticity.

Artery. A blood vessel that carries blood from the heart to various parts of the body.

Artificial heart. Any mechanical device designed to replace the heart on either a permanent or temporary basis.

Atherosclerosis. A form of arteriosclerosis in which the inner walls of the arteries become thick with fatty deposits.

Atrium. One of the two upper chambers of the heart. The chief function of the atrium is to receive blood from the veins. The plural of atrium is *atria.*

Blood pressure. The force of blood on the walls of the arteries. Systolic pressure is the force of the blood on the

[118]

arteries when the heart is contracting. Diastolic pressure is the force on the arteries when the heart is at rest.

Capillaries. The smallest blood vessels in the body. The capillaries carry blood from the arteries to the veins. Oxygen and carbon dioxide pass in and out of the blood through the thin walls of the capillaries.

Cardiac. Anything to do with the heart.

Cardiac arrest. A halt in heartbeat, leading to a stop in the blood circulation and usually to death.

Cardiology. The medical study of the heart and how it works. The physician who is a specialist in cardiology is known as a *cardiologist.*

Cardiomyopathy. A serious disease of unknown cause that results in the inability of the heart muscles to pump sufficient blood.

Cardiovascular. Anything to do with the heart and the blood vessels.

Circulatory system. The heart and blood vessels, and the movement of the blood.

Clot. A solid mass of blood. Some clots can block blood vessels, cutting off the blood flow.

Coronary arteries. Arteries that branch off from the aorta and supply blood to the heart muscles. The coronary arteries have several branches.

Coronary bypass. An operation to improve the blood supply to the heart muscles when clogged coronary arteries reduce the flow. The usual procedure is to take blood vessels from the patient's leg and graft them in place to carry the blood around the blocked coronary artery.

Graft. In medicine, the transfer of living tissue from one place to another or from one person to another. If the graft is successful, the grafted tissue will grow in its new location.

Heart attack. A popular term for myocardial infarction. *See also* Myocardial infarction.

Heart-lung machine. A device that takes over the action of the heart during open-heart surgery. The heart-lung machine adds oxygen to the blood before the blood is returned to the body.

[119]

Heart transplant. Replacing a diseased or damaged heart with a healthy heart from someone who has just died.

Inferior vena cava. See Vena cava.

Mitral valve. The structure between the left atrium and the left ventricle that allows the blood to flow in only one direction without backing up.

Muscle. Tissue that can contract and expand to cause movement or exert force.

Myocardial infarction. The medical term for heart attack. The condition results from a reduced flow of blood to the heart muscles caused by the blockage of a blood vessel. The patient suffers considerable pain as affected heart muscles are damaged or killed.

Pericardium. The thin, but tough, lining that completely covers the heart.

Semilunar valves. The structures that are located between the right ventricle and the pulmonary artery and between the left ventricle and the aorta. The valves allow the blood to flow in only one direction and prevent backing up.

Septum. The up-and-down wall of muscle that separates the heart chambers of the left side of the heart from those on the right side.

Superior vena cava. See Vena cava.

Thrombosis. A blood clot that blocks a blood vessel.

Tricuspid valve. The structure between the right atrium and right ventricle of the heart. It regulates the one-way flow of the blood with no slipping or backward motion.

Vein. A blood vessel that carries blood from various parts of the body back to the heart.

Vena cava. The largest vein of the body. It returns blood from the parts of the body to the right atrium of the heart. It is divided into two veins, the superior vena cava and the inferior vena cava.

Ventricle. One of the two lower chambers of the heart. The ventricles pump the blood to the lungs and to all the parts of the body.

Venules. Small veins that branch off from larger veins.

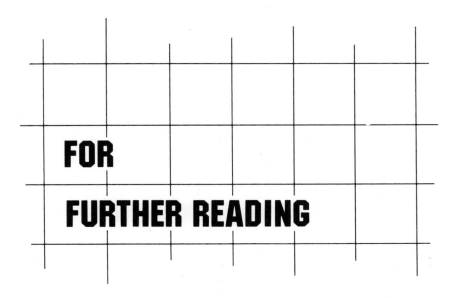

FOR

FURTHER READING

Chung, Edward K. *One Heart, One Life*. Englewood Cliffs, N.J.: Prentice Hall, 1982.

Comroe, Julius H. *Exploring the Heart*. New York: Norton, 1983.

DeBakey, Michael E., and Antonio Gotto. *The Living Heart*. New York: McKay, 1977.

Fox, Renee C., and Judith P. Swazey. *The Courage to Fail*. Chicago: University of Chicago, 1974.

Leinwald, Gerald. *Transplants*. New York: Franklin Watts, 1985.

Moore, Francis D. *Transplant*. New York: Simon & Schuster, 1972.

Shaw, Margery W., ed. *After Barney Clark*. Austin: University of Texas, 1984.

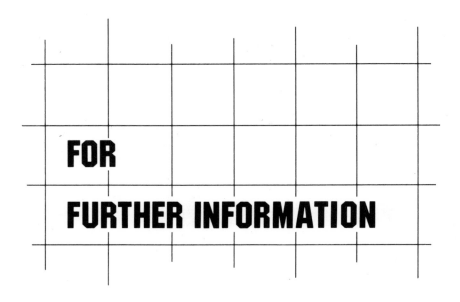

FOR

FURTHER INFORMATION

American Heart Association
7320 Greenville Avenue
Dallas, TX 75231

International Society for Heart Transplants
Thoracic and Cardiovascular Surgery
Newark Beth Israel Hospital
201 Lyons Avenue
Newark, NJ 07112

Information Office
National Heart, Lung, and Blood Institute
National Institutes of Health
9000 Rockville Pike
Bethesda, MD 20205

[122]

LIST OF
SOURCES

MEDICAL JOURNALS

Circulation, December 1983, "Cardiac Transplants and the Artificial Heart"; September 1985, "The Role of Mechanical Support and Transplantation"

Heart Transplantation, May 1984, "Heart Transplantation for End-Stage Ischemic Heart Disease"

Journal of the American Medical Association, February 10, 1981, "Implantable Assist Pump"

Journal of Cardiovascular Medicine, July 1981, "Left Ventricular Assist Pumps and the Artificial Heart"; October 1983, "The Artificial Heart"

The New England Journal of Medicine, July 14, 1983, "Transplantation"; February 2, 1984, "Clinical Use of the Total Artificial Heart"; "Political History of the Artificial Heart"; "Ethical Issues in the Implantation of the Total Artificial Heart"; March 29, 1984, "The Politics of Transplantation"; November 29, 1984, "Heart Transplantation After 16 Years"

Postgraduate Medicine, November 15, 1985, "Cardiac Transplantation"

BOOKS

The books used as sources are listed in "For Further Reading."

MAGAZINES AND NEWSPAPERS

Cardio News, January 1985, "A New Life for the Artificial Heart"; November/December 1985, "Progress and Problems in Heart-Lung Transplants"

Consumer Research, May 1986, "Vital Facts About Organ Transplants"

Discover, February 1983, "Replacing the Heart"; June 1986, "The Artificial Heart Is Really Very Dangerous"

Health, April 1984, "The Lessons from Barney Clark's Heart"

Medical World News, January 10, 1983, "Pneumatic Heart"; February 11, 1985, "The Artificial Heart Controversy"; April 8, 1985, "The Phoenix Heart"; May 27, 1985, "Artificial Hearts"

New York Times, December 3, 1982, "Dentist, Close to Death, Receives First Permanent Artificial Heart"; March 25, 1983, "Dr. Clark's Death Laid to Failure of All Organs"; June 5, 1983, "Ethics and the New Medicine"; November 19, 1985, "Appraising the Artificial Heart: Days of Doubt"; December 3, 1985, "Artificial Heart: Should It Be Scaled Back?"; August 10, 1986, "A Hero of Medicine"

Psychology Today, October 1984, "Transplant Surgery"

Quest, June 1981, "A Change of Heart"

Scientific American, January 1981, "The Total Artificial Heart"

Time, December 13, 1982, "Living on Borrowed Time"; April 4, 1983, "Death of a Gallant Pioneer"; April 11, 1983, "Debate on the Boundary of Life"; November 11, 1985, "Bridging the Gap"

GOVERNMENT PUBLICATIONS

Published by the National Institutes of Health of the Department of Health and Human Services:

"Artificial Heart and Assist Devices," May 1985

"The Heart: Diagnosis and Treatment," November 1980

"High Blood Pressure," December 1980

"The Lungs," July 1979

"National Heart, Lung, and Blood Institute's Fact Book for Fiscal Year 1980," October 1980

Additional sources include personal communications from the University of Utah Medical Center, the Milton S. Hershey Medical Center of Pennsylvania State University, and the Office of Organ Transplantation of the Department of Health and Human Services.

INDEX